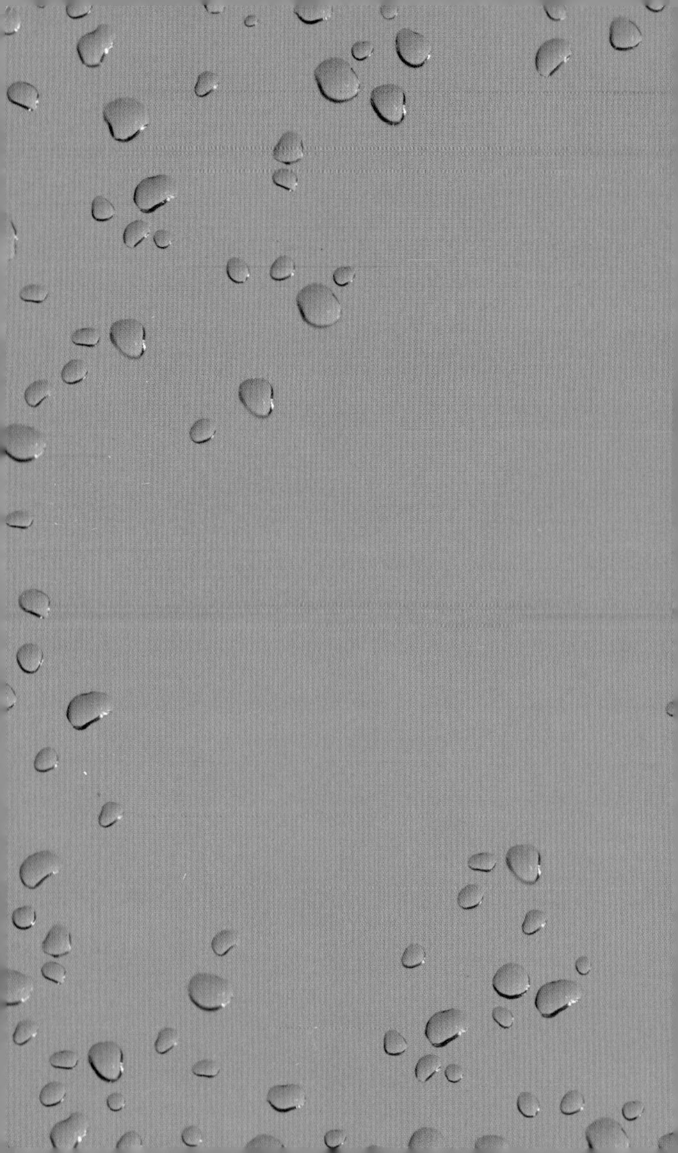

Catch of the Day

JIMMY HOUSTON

COUNTRYMAN®
A Division of Thomas Nelson Publishers

THOMAS NELSON®
Since 1798

NASHVILLE DALLAS MEXICO CITY RIO DE JANEIRO

Published in Nashville, Tennessee, by Thomas Nelson. Thomas Nelson is a registered trademark of Thomas Nelson, Inc.

Thomas Nelson, Inc., titles may be purchased in bulk for educational, business, fund-raising, or sales promotional use. For information, please e-mail SpecialMarkets@ThomasNelson.com.

ISBN: 978-1-4003-1964-0

Printed in China
16 WAI 6

January

JANUARY 1

GENESIS 1:1

In the beginning God created the sky and the earth.

IT'S ALWAYS EXCITING to begin something new like a new job, new house, new marriage, or a new family. New projects excite and energize me. I'm always excited about beginning a new tournament season where all the fishermen start out again at zero. I can't wait for the start of Major League Baseball or the first game of Oklahoma University football or basketball.

TIP

Use the cold winter months to clean and organize all your tackle to get ready for that great spring fishin'.

One tradition I started more than thirty-five years ago was to begin each January 1 and read the Bible through in a year. Now, I've completely read the Bible through more than thirty times, in addition to my other Bible reading and study. Start your very own tradition today. Five, ten, twenty years from now, you'll be amazed at what God wants to tell you on a daily basis.

January 2

GENESIS 1:27

So God created human beings in his image.

God could have made us look like anything He wanted. We could have looked like the space aliens we see on *Star Trek* or *Men in Black*. We could have looked like frogs, or fish, or anything else God chose. But He chose to pattern us after Himself. We are patterned after God—physically, emotionally, and spiritually. We are not God, we are not perfect, but we are patterned to be that way.

The next time you have a pity party about how you look or feel, think about what God could have made you look like and how He could have made you feel. Then look in that mirror and smile. Look inside yourself and laugh; God patterned you and me after Himself!

TIP

Spool on new line at the start of every year and every four to six weeks during fishin' season.

JANUARY 3

PROVERBS 10:2

Riches gotten by doing wrong have no value,
but right living will save you from death.

FISHING TOURNAMENTS have brought out the very best and very worst in fishermen. While tournaments are incredibly fair and honest, cheating does creep in sometimes. Blatant cheating is usually discovered quickly, and cheaters are disqualified, generally banned for life. Unintentional rule breaking is punished by penalties, such as a weight penalty or loss of your catch for that day.

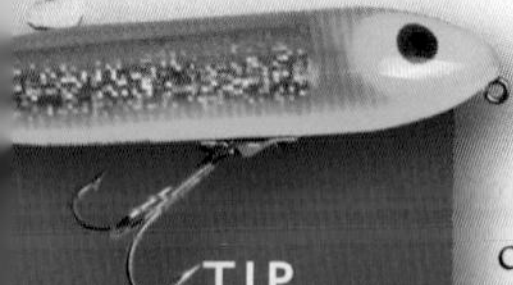

TIP
Bass are not very aggressive in cold water. Use slow-moving baits and be patient.

The most damaging cheaters are the ones who bend the rules for their own benefit and ill-gotten gain. These anglers are bending or breaking the rules with almost no chance of ever being caught. But those gains will never last. Opportunities for ill-gotten gain come into our lives all the time. While we may never be caught, our very life may depend on how we handle these temptations to cheat.

January 4

LUKE 12:34

Your heart will be where your treasure is.

EVERY FISHERMAN has a favorite bait. For me, it's a Booyah spinnerbait for bass and a Road Runner for crappie. Single baits, but within each bait category is a wide variety of colors, sizes, and even different types of materials. I treasure these baits because I can have success in just about every situation.

If our treasure is Jesus, we have a God we can rely on in all of life's situations. If our thoughts are on Jesus, we become a better friend, coworker, husband, or wife. We also become more a likable, friendlier person even to strangers!

TIP

Slow rolling a white spinnerbait with a large Oklahoma blade works great for lethargic wintertime bass.

JANUARY 5

PSALM 31:24

All you who put your hope in the LORD
be strong and brave.

BETTER FISHERMEN do not hope for success or rely on luck in order to catch fish. They pin their hopes on facts, skills, knowledge, and experience. The more of these we have, the more fish we catch and the more consistent we become.

Similarly, the more we know and experience about Jesus, the better we will be at becoming the kind of person we want to be and God wants us to be. This doesn't happen overnight. It takes time to become a great fisherman. So be strong; it also takes time for God to mold us into the person we will become. The great part is that God allows us the opportunity to become better every day we stay close to Him.

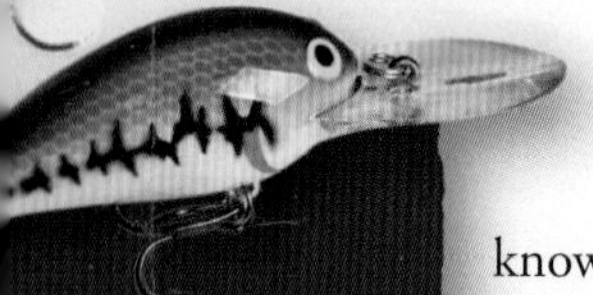

TIP
Pork trailers on jigs and spinnerbaits work better than soft plastics in cold water.

MATTHEW 28:20

"I will be with you always, even until the end of this age."

FISHING IS A SPORT most enjoyed with someone else. Sure, we can fish alone and have fun, but it is always more enjoyable with a friend or another member of your family. My closest fishin' partner is my wife, Chris. My most memorable days fishin' are not great tournament victories, but days spent with her or fishin' with my kids or grandkids.

God never intended for us to be alone. That's why He sent Jesus. That is why when we are saved, God places His Holy Spirit in us. No matter how isolated or alone we may feel at times, Jesus is always there. All we need to do is call on Him.

TIP

Vertical jig your Road Runners during the winter months to catch more crappie.

January 7

PROVERBS 10:22

The Lord's blessing brings wealth,
and no sorrow comes with it.

THE OTHER DAY, I asked a guy in another boat, "I wonder what the poor people are doing today?" He answered, "They're fishing."

Fishing is one of those blessings from God that makes us rich, no matter what our bank account says. Too often, though, we dwell on the sorrows the devil throws at us rather than the blessings we have. This is exactly what the devil wants; he's working to ruin our day and our life.

TIP

Lighter line is more manageable in cold conditions and will get you more bites.

As Christians and children of God, we cannot accept that. Today, write down ten or fifteen of the blessings God has placed in your life. Before you get halfway done, the devil will be hard-pressed to have a chance to ruin your day. By the way, this little trick will work again tomorrow.

January 8

PSALM 86:5

Lord, you are kind and forgiving
and have great love for those who call to you.

FISHERMEN since the beginning of time have been asking for help and advice on how to catch more fish. Jesus told Peter where to cast his net, and some of us today make our living telling others how to become better fishermen. I know people who have driven hundreds of miles to listen to a top tournament pro give a seminar. They do this just to be more successful on the water.

God is the ultimate expert, and He is ready and willing to answer our questions and to come to our aid. All we need to do is ask. But somehow—out of "macho-ness," lack of faith, or whatever—we'll not come to God and ask until it's the last resort. But if we'll get God involved in today's problems and concerns right now, we'll likely not need to use God as the last resort tomorrow.

TIP

Standing treetops often hold bass in clear water lakes throughout the winter months.

2 TIMOTHY 3:16

All Scripture is inspired by God and is useful for teaching, for showing people what is wrong in their lives, for correcting faults, and for teaching how to live right.

We're allowed three days to practice for a BASS (Bass Anglers Sportsman Society) tournament.

Most competitors will tell you this is the time to locate the fish and to figure out what lures and tactics will work best in order to have success during the actual competition. Just as important, however, is learning the places where you cannot catch fish and what baits won't work!

TIP

Fish where muddy water and clear water are mixing together.

When God's Word (the Bible) is read and spoken (preached), it lays out what God will do for us. It also directly focuses on problem areas in our lives. Open the Bible anywhere and start reading, God will soon tell you about changes you need to make to improve your life, and then He'll help you make those changes. God loves us so much, He wants to make us better every day.

January 10

PSALM 14:2

The Lord looked down from heaven on all people.

We wear polarized sunglasses when fishing in order to be able to see down into the water. Polarization removes the glare from the surface and allows us to see a foot or two or even more into clear water. This is helpful. We can see stumps, rocks, logs, and other hiding places for the fish. We sometimes can even see the fish!

It's pretty awesome that God can see us all and yet focus on each of us individually. How would we treat our family, friends, or even perfect strangers if we knew God was there looking over our shoulders? Well, He is! Keep this in mind today when someone messes up your order at the drive-through, disappoints you, or cuts you off in traffic. Live today trying to please God . . . you just might do it!

TIP

Remember to visit a heated fishing dock for a very comfortable wintertime crappie outing.

January 11

2 THESSALONIANS 1:11

That is why we always pray for you, asking our God to help you live the kind of life he called you to live.

Competition breeds prayer. I believe almost all tournament fishermen pray, even the non-Christians. Most of the time, when we pray, we're praying for our own glory. We're asking God to do something special, something supernatural for us.

TIP

Steeper banks will yield more fish during the cold winter months.

Today, direct your energy into praying for someone else. Lift up your family, friends, pastor, and coworkers. Pray for that person at the drive-through window and even for your enemies or someone who has done you wrong. It's pretty difficult for me to pray for someone who has wronged me, but when I do, God creates some peace in my heart where before there was pain. Dedicate your prayers today to others, and your God will receive the glory.

January 12

EXODUS 20:3

You must not have any other gods except me.

For many people, their passion about something becomes their religion. Fishing is one of those passions that can become almost a religious experience.

I don't know how many times I've heard someone talk about getting closer to God on the lake. Others tell me they can worship God better on the lake on Sunday than in church with a bunch of Christians who might be hypocrites. But when we do this, we're not worshiping God at all. We're making fishing our god. At the very least, we're guilty of worshiping God's creation. This is really the same as worshiping the moon or the stars. God commands us to assemble to worship Him and Him only!

TIP

A shad die-off in extremely cold weather will trigger good bass fishing.

January 13

JAMES 1:12

When people are tempted and still continue strong, they should be happy. After they have proved their faith, God will reward them with life forever.

"WHY ME, LORD?" How often have we all uttered these words in times of struggle or testing? I wonder sometimes on the lake how many things can go wrong. "If this is a test, Lord, I'd rather take a written one!" We can either react to these trials with frustration, anger, and even foul language, or we can react with patience. God promises to bless us when we patiently endure.

TIP

Check the diameter of your fishing line. Different lines have different diameters, even in the same pound tests.

A day of fishing is seldom perfect, just like a day doing anything else is seldom perfect. How we handle those breakdowns, or tests, is what is important. We can be patient and be blessed, or we can blow it—and what does that really accomplish anyway?

January 14

PSALM 33:7

He gathered the water of the sea into a heap.
He made the great ocean stay in its place.

LAKESIDE VIEWS. Desktop fountains. Backyard ponds. Water captivates us all, and it is, of course, even more important to fishermen. We really can't help but have a love affair with water, but do we have that same fascination and love for the awesome God who created and controls that water?

When I look at a lake, river, or stream, I'm always reminded of how much God loves us to create something we enjoy so much. I also realize that God has set boundaries on how we are to live our lives. Those boundaries are for our own good. Living within God's boundaries not only pleases Him, it keeps us out of all sorts of calamities and sin.

TIP

Seek out the clearer water areas when water temperatures are low.

January 15

MARK 2:10

"But I will prove to you that the Son of Man has authority on earth to forgive sins."

SOMETIMES talk is big during practice rounds at bass tournaments. Even when fishermen fail to catch much on tournament day, they still brag about all the big ones they caught in practice. The real proof comes when they carry those bass to the weigh-in scales.

TIP

Slightly open up the hook on your spinnerbait for better hookups and fewer missed bass!

Jesus claimed authority to forgive sins. He backed this up by making the blind see, the lame walk, and the dead come back to life. He ultimately backed this up by His death on the cross and His resurrection three days later. He then walked among the living here on earth for forty more days. Jesus can and will forgive our sins if we ask Him. He will also carry us to that great weigh-in in heaven!

January 16

MARK 4:25

"Those who have understanding will be given more."

WITHOUT A DOUBT, knowledge and understanding are the keys to becoming a better fisherman. The fisherman who "knows it all" will very seldom develop into a consistent fish catcher. Those who are open to instruction and criticism will become champions.

TIP

Fish always face into the current. Cast your bait upstream, and let it flow into the fish's position.

We open ourselves up to God's teaching by praying consistently and then by receiving the ways God answers those prayers. If we're consistent in acting within what God says to do, we'll gain more understanding about Him and His direction for our lives. This direction will become evident to our family and friends, and it will even be seen by folks we don't know. Develop a daily, consistent prayer life, and your relationship with God and your understanding of Him will grow on a daily basis.

January 17

PSALM 37:3

Trust the Lord and do good.

I FINISHED THIRD in a BASS tournament on Lake Powell, Arizona. Fred Ward won, Larry Nixon was second, and we were all fishing 113 miles or so from takeoff and weigh-in. To travel 113 miles, one way, was putting a tremendous amount of trust in that big Mercury outboard. By placing trust in that motor, I did well. We all did well, and we prospered.

TIP

After a cold front, try a white Marabou Road Runner with a fluorescent red head.

No matter what, we can't fail when we place our trust in the God who created us. We're not always going to prosper in everything we do. We will falter at times, but I know this: I have victory and safety and prosperity in Jesus, regardless of what might go wrong today. This trust in Him will carry me safely through.

MATTHEW 13:41

"The Son of Man will send out his angels, and they will gather out of his kingdom all who cause sin and all who do evil."

Ray Scott, the founder of the Bass Anglers Sportsman Society, has a great belief that angels have been a big part of his life and have played a major part in the startup and growth of BASS He believes God has sent humans as angels to assist him in times of need.

The Bible teaches of angels and promises that God will provide angels for the protection of His people. He will also use angels to do away with all the causes of sin. There will come a time when everything on earth will be made perfect. There will be no need for news reports that dwell on Earth's problems, because there will be no problems. This is the Good News for all who have Jesus Christ as their personal Savior.

TIP

Use translucent soft plastics in clear water. You can almost see through them.

January 19

PSALM 18:1

I love you, Lord. You are my strength.

Tournament bass fishing is a much more physical sport than most nontournament fishermen realize. Most of us do not carry a front seat in our boat, so we have to stand constantly while fishing. I do not eat or drink anything during competition hours. Tournaments also usually allow very little time for sleep. You need strength to endure.

TIP
Spray Reel Magic on your reels two or three times every day to give you more casting distance.

Whether or not you are a believer, your strength in every aspect of life comes from God. He has divinely made us to do almost miraculous things. No machine, robot, or even that Energizer Bunny® can keep going the way we can. Today, pay special attention to the physical abilities God has given you to just keep going and going. Thank Him for this, and give Him your praise and love.

January 20

EXODUS 18:20

Warn them about the laws and teachings, and teach them the right way to live and what they should do.

Fishing is a sport where our results are determined by the decisions we make. Every day on the water, we make hundreds of decisions. Sometimes we might have to choose between only two or three options, while other times we might have to select from two or three hundred possibilities. Seldom will we make the very best decision each time. The trick is to make more decisions that are on the better side than on the worse side. These are *our* decisions.

We are told to conduct our lives based on God's decisions, laws, and instruction. Why should we do this? Because God's decisions will always produce the very best results in our lives. This is true for all aspects of life, including our families, our jobs, our spare time, even our eating habits. God truly does know what is best for us!

TIP

Fish directly below dams and spillways for great white bass, striper, and catfish action.

January 21

LUKE 8:39

"Go back home and tell people how much God has done for you."

Some fishing patterns are like the seasons: they are only productive during a short time. For example, the spawn only last a few weeks, so fishing for bedding fish is a short-term opportunity. The time that fish actively school is usually just a short period each year. Certain lures are supereffective only a few weeks each year.

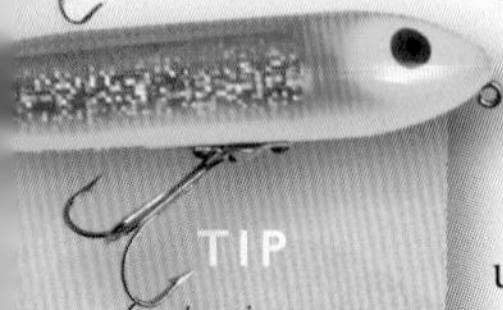

TIP
Customize your lures by adding a little red to them.

Jesus spent a mere thirty-three years on Earth about two thousand years ago. He repeatedly told those whom He encountered to tell others about their experiences with Him. He wanted to make sure we knew who He was, why He came, and especially how much He loves us, our families, and our friends.

This Jesus, our Savior, the One we trust and depend on to get us to heaven and eternal life, is now depending on us to tell others how much He has done for you and me. Be sure to tell someone today.

JANUARY 22

PROVERBS 25:28

Those who do not control themselves are like a city whose walls are broken down.

FISHING A SPINNERBAIT is all about control. The best spinnerbait fisherman is the one who can control the bait. This begins with great casting accuracy, but it also includes retrieval speed, depth, and even angles of presentation.

Controlling our temper, words, thoughts, and actions on a daily basis can be a real challenge. When we lose our self-control, we say and do things we later regret. Not to mention it drives our blood pressure sky high. The easiest way to maintain self-control is to live each day as close to God as we can. I try to do this by praying a lot, thanking and praising God in my prayers. Listening to praise and gospel music also helps. If we are concentrating on our God, then we'll have less trouble controlling ourselves.

TIP

Use a coffee cup or coffee can to practice your casting on days when you can't go fishin'.

January 23

JAMES 3:8

No one can tame the tongue.

The most identifiable way to tell the difference between a largemouth bass and a spotted bass is the tongue. Spotted bass have a patch of teeth on their tongue. When you rub your finger over the tongue, the teeth are very easy to feel.

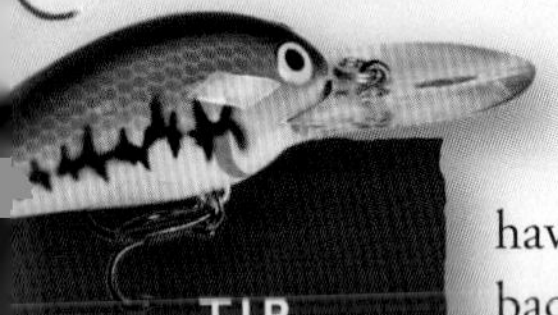

TIP

Fish prefer rocky banks in the winter because the rocks give more heat.

It seems that most of us have fangs on our tongues at times. The bad thing is once we have said something, we can't take it back. Perhaps just as evil as speaking something bad *to* someone is saying bad things *about* someone.

The devil uses gossip to destroy relationships. He makes it fun to spread a little dirt and exaggerate the facts. I pray every day to have God keep me from saying anything bad about anyone. I fail often, but God isn't finished with me.

January 24

PHILIPPIANS 4:8

Brothers and sisters, think about the things that are good and worthy of praise. Think about the things that are true and honorable and right and pure and beautiful and respected.

BASS TOURNAMENT FISHERMEN are some of the most focused of all competitors. We must concentrate for long periods of time, and if we lose that concentration, even for just a cast or two, it can cost us dearly.

As men and women of God, we are instructed to concentrate on all the good things God puts in our lives. Why? If we concentrate on these, we'll most likely act upon these thoughts. We will be treating others the way God intends us to treat them.

If our thoughts are dishonorable and evil instead, we are apt to act on these thoughts in our relationships. Of course, this does not please God, but pleases the devil instead. Think of something pure, honorable, or lovely . . . right now!

TIP

Ponds warm up two to three weeks earlier than large reservoirs, making for great early season fishing.

January 25

2 TIMOTHY 1:12

I am not ashamed, because I know Jesus, the One in whom I have believed. And I am sure he is able to protect what he has trusted me with until that day.

Fishermen rely on information from others to help us plan our fishin' trips. We look at lake levels and conditions, read fishing reports, and even call our friends to find out where the fish are biting and what they are biting on.

TIP

Live bait often will catch fish in cold weather when artificial bait fail.

All I need to know about life as a born-again Christian is in God's Word, the Bible. And the greatest Friend I have is Jesus Christ. While fishing information may be sketchy, outdated, or just downright wrong, God's information never changes and never has errors. God's Word promises that Jesus will return. I have entrusted to Him my very soul, and most importantly I've entrusted it to Him for eternity.

January 26

PROVERBS 27:9

The sweet smell of perfume and oils is pleasant,
and so is good advice from a friend.

TOURNAMENT ANGLERS seldom go it alone during competition. Most have one or two close friends to confide in as they try to solve the mysteries of how to succeed on any given lake. We trust that our friends want our success just as much as their own.

In the same way, a Christian's main source of counsel should be pastors, deacons, and the rest of the church family. This is one of the very great benefits of belonging to, attending, and working in God's church. Many individuals who claim Christianity and claim Jesus as their Lord and Savior do not participate in a local church, but according to God's Word, this is not what He intended. God built His church for His people to be involved in for their mutual benefit and for His glory.

TIP

Mid- to late afternoons are better for winter fishin'.

January 27

PSALM 108:13

We can win with God's help.

EGO IS A GREAT STUMBLING BLOCK for most of us. It can hurt us in our attempts to catch fish, and it can impede just about anything else we try to accomplish. That ego inside of us just presses on to make us want to do it all on our own. That's not God's way. He wants to help; in fact, He even insists on helping.

TIP

A 10-inch or 11-inch worm works well in lakes with lots of grass.

The children of Israel succeeded at every turn when they depended on God's help, but they failed miserably when they acted on their own without God's help. Even with these examples, we try to do things our way and call on God only when our way fails. Why not call on God first? What does God want to help with? Everything. From the smallest part of our lives to the most important.

JANUARY 28

PSALM 119:30

I have chosen the way of truth;
I have obeyed your laws.

ONE OF THE MOST difficult things for me in fishing and hunting is to know the laws in each state I am in. I once got a citation after a show aired on television. We were catfishing with Yo-Bobs, which are kind of like jug lining. Kansas law requires these to be anchored to the bottom of the lake. I had called the local game ranger and asked him what the laws were, but he either didn't know or failed to mention this anchoring part. His boss, who saw the show, knew the law, and both the ranger and I were in trouble.

TIP

A five-foot ultralight rod will make even the smallest of fish fun to catch.

God's laws are simple yet straightforward. He tells us these laws in His Word, and He actually writes these laws on our hearts. He does this because His laws are for our benefit. What an awesome God!

January 29

JAMES 4:7

So give yourselves completely to God. Stand against the devil, and the devil will run from you.

I'VE SEEN some tournament competitors become downright obnoxious when they were doing well and placing high or winning. Tournament fishing, however, has a way of humbling everyone, no matter who you are or how much you've won.

God loves humility and the devil hates it. God hates arrogance and the devil loves it. The devil will spend a great deal of time trying to convince us how great we are, what a great thing we did, or how much we have accomplished. Not only is such pride a sin, but it undoubtedly will carry a price tag with it. Jesus humbled Himself to the point of dying on the cross. He washed the feet of His disciples and lowered Himself to the position of servant at every opportunity. What a great example for you and me!

TIP

Going to the upper ends of creeks and rivers is the easiest way to locate fish on unfamiliar lakes.

JEREMIAH 31:33

I will put my teachings in their minds
and write them on their hearts.

SOME PEOPLE just seem to be born with the ability to catch fish. I've often said that Chris (my wife), Roland Martin, and Larry Nixon are the most natural-born anglers I have ever fished with. They all have an amazing, God-given talent to figure out how to catch fish. Sure, they have great skills, but they also have that extra sense about fishing that most other anglers—including me—don't possess.

TIP
Evergreen trees make excellent structure to place in your favorite fishin' hole.

God has promised to place in us an extraordinary sense so that we may know in our minds and feel in our hearts exactly what we need to do and think to please Him. All we must do is follow and obey. The result will be the great blessings God has promised. I fail often, but praise God He has written these laws with a permanent marker!

JANUARY 31

EPHESIANS 4:29

When you talk, do not say harmful things, but say what people need—words that will help others become stronger.

BOB FERRIS was the best bass tournament announcer of all time. He announced Bass'n Gals tournaments for all twenty-one years of the organization. Yes, he had a big, booming voice and tremendous stage presence, but what made him great was what he said and the way he said it. He made all the women feel important and always encouraged them just enough to make them believe they had a great chance to catch fish and do well in the tournaments.

TIP

Always wet your knots before cinching them down.

In daily life, if each of us went about trying to be helpful and encourage those with whom we come in contact, the whole world would be a better place to live. Not only that, we would be encouraged and helped by those around us.

February

February 1

PSALM 90:12

Teach us how short our lives really are
so that we may be wise.

TOURNAMENT FISHING is not only an effort to catch bass; it's a monumental struggle against time. Perhaps our most important use of time is the three days we have to practice for a tournament. If we use that time wisely, we'll probably have a great tournament.

TIP
Always make sure your crankbait or jerkbait is running perfectly straight.

God says that using our time well will grow our wisdom. I believe that God wants us to go about doing things that are important to Him. Some of our time every day must be spent praying (talking to God). Some time must be spent in God's Word (God talking to us). Some of our time must be used to tell others what Jesus is doing in our lives (talking about God). I know I need to grow in wisdom and am thankful God has a plan for me to do just that.

PROVERBS 13:21

Trouble always comes to sinners,
but good people enjoy success.

SOME DAYS we feel like we are walking under a cloud that rains only on us. Our boat won't start, the fish won't bite, we break a rod, and so forth. One trouble simply leads to another.

Sometimes much of life seems just like that. Mostly, we blame others or other situations, but God tells us our sins may be creating our problems. If trouble chases sinners, then trouble will catch up most of the time, if not all the time. That's the bad news. The good news is that God is ready, willing, and able to forgive these sins. When we repent of these sins and ask God's forgiveness, He erases our wrongness and replaces it with the righteousness of Jesus. What chases us then is the abundance of God's blessings.

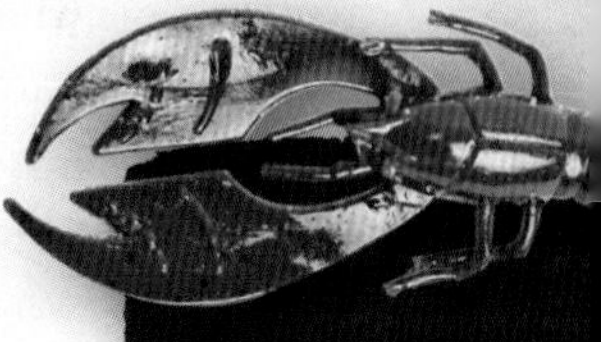

TIP

Blue and red are the basic colors that bass can see best.

February 3

LUKE 21:19

"By continuing to have faith you will save your lives."

Jesus told those words to His disciples after warning them that they would be persecuted for their allegiance to Him. This verse helped strengthen me when I was chastised for refusing to wear a beer patch on my tournament shirt or place a beer brand decal on my boat. Not only was I criticized by non-Christians, but by Christian fishermen as well. My stand against promoting or selling alcohol is a longstanding one. We own a big convenience and tackle store on Lake Tenkiller in Oklahoma, where we have never sold beer. I'm told that this position costs me $40,000 per year in profit.

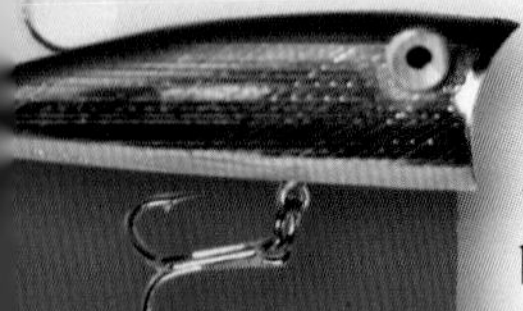

TIP

Use backing when filling your casting reels with new line. This will save you money and time.

Jesus told us to stand firm. We can't put a price tag on what we believe, and Jesus has already paid the price for our souls. So . . . stand firm.

FEBRUARY 4

JOSHUA 24:15

As for me and my family, we will serve the LORD.

CHOICES ABOUND in fishing. From the moment we even start to think about going fishing, we start making choices. Making those choices is part of the fun in fishing, and the better the choices, the better the fishing and the fishing trip.

TIP

Willow leaf blades produce better in clear water.

We have only one choice to make about Jesus: we either believe in Him or we don't. Our choice not only makes a tremendous difference in our trip through this life, but it makes a difference for eternity. That difference is heaven or hell!

Whom will you serve today? What about your family? We have so many choices today, but any choice other than serving the Lord will end in complete failure.

February 5

PROVERBS 1:18

But sinners will fall into their own traps;
they will only catch themselves!

NO ONE LIKES to be told they've messed up, made a mistake, or failed. Over the years, ESPN has told us what they see wrong in our televised fishing shows. We can't ignore that criticism, so we accept it and work double hard to make the show better, even if we believe we're right and they are wrong. The result is generally a better show.

TIP

The colder the water, the slower you need to work your lures.

The next time someone criticizes you, use it to your advantage. According to God's Word, the trick is to accept it. Don't ignore it, don't make excuses, and don't argue about it. Accept the criticism and look for a positive way to build upon it. That will bring success and honor.

PSALM 112:5

It is good to be merciful and generous.

LURES CAN get pretty expensive on the water. I've told many a partner I've got one more lure just like the one I'm catching fish on, but it will really cost them. Seriously, almost any fisherman will give a hot lure to his partner. At a BASS tournament one year on Lake Guntersville in Alabama, I gave my partner the jerkbait, rod, reel, line, and everything I had just caught my limit on. He could not believe it, but I wanted him to catch fish.

God expects and intends for us to be generous not only with our money, but also our time. When we give of ourselves and our resources, we will always receive much more in return. That return might not be immediate, but it will definitely come about in God's good time.

TIP

Check your rod tips and guides periodically for breaks or cracks that can damage your line.

February 7

PROVERBS 19:21

People can make all kinds of plans,
but only the Lord's plan will happen.

When we started the Bible study at the tournaments back in 1983, I had no idea what God had in store. This Bible study group quickly turned into FOCAS, the Fellowship of Christian Anglers Society.

I knew I was missing a lot of church during fishing tournaments, and I still needed fellowship with other Christians. God's purpose was much larger . . . saving lost souls and changing lives! Almost thirty years later, there are FOCAS meetings at most major tournament events. Praise God that I followed His leadership with my actions. Whatever you do today, include God in all of your plans. He has a purpose for everything you do, and His purpose is not only the best, but it will prevail!

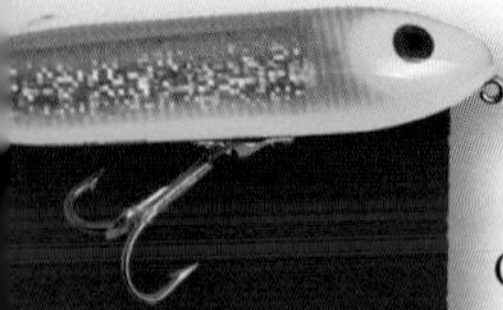

TIP
Develop a simple game plan for each day's tournament.

ROMANS 7:6

So now we serve God in a new way with the Spirit, and not in the old way with written rules.

FISHING HAS CHANGED so much over the last several years. Most of the hot lures today were not even around as few as three or four years ago. All of our equipment is so much better. These new ways to fish have certainly made the game better.

Jesus has brought about the new way to serve God. He re-explained the law and put His Spirit and commandments in our hearts. We worship out of thanks and praise for what Jesus has done for each of us. Worship Him today by demonstrating His love to everyone you meet. Praise Him by letting His Spirit guide you in every situation you're involved in. Now, let's serve God in all we do.

TIP

Early season sport shows are a great place to learn more about fishing. Attend every seminar.

February 9

1 CORINTHIANS 10:13

The only temptation that has come to you is that which everyone has. But you can trust God, who will not permit you to be tempted more than you can stand.

EVEN THE MOST honest of all tournament fishermen will still have situations come up that will allow them to bend the rules. These are temptations, and I believe they come from the devil. We're told that everyone is attacked by these temptations, but as children of God, we always have a way out. That way out can come in many forms, but I believe the easiest way out is simple prayer.

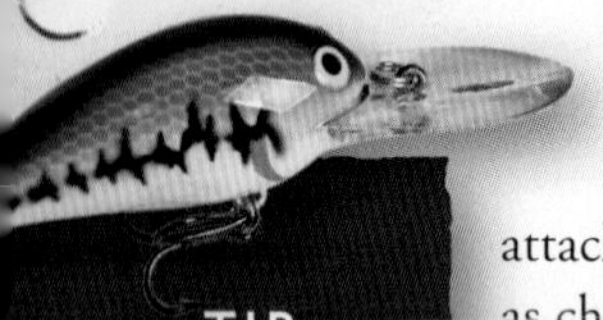

TIP

Tip your Road Runner with a live minnow when fishing is extremely tough.

No matter how attractive the devil makes temptations look, don't forget or neglect to pray your way out. Ask God to show you the way and, according to His promise, He will.

ACTS 13:38

Through Jesus everyone who believes is free from all sins.

ONE YEAR, my wife, Chris, won so much during the Bass'n Gals tournaments, she actually began to feel guilty about winning. I really believe she lost the Bass'n Gals Classic that year because of those guilt feelings. (She claims that's not true.)

Of course, we shouldn't feel guilty about winning.

We carry a huge burden of guilt for the sinful things we do in our lives. This burden can affect all aspects of our daily lives. Belief in Jesus will free us of that guilt. This is what God's gospel is about, removing the guilt and declaring us right with almighty God. This gives you and me the freedom to make the most out of every day God gives us—free from guilt, free from sin, and right with God.

TIP

Fish close to the shoreline when fishing ponds (or tanks, as they are called in Texas).

FEBRUARY 11

PSALM 91:11

He has put his angels in charge of you
to watch over you wherever you go.

OVER THE YEARS, I've had many close calls on the water. One came when I was sixteen years old, baiting a trotline at night in February. I was with my good friend Bobby Ballew, and the water was icy cold. Our boat capsized with only the nose remaining above the water. We had just enough room to put one finger each in the bow eye and hold on and yell for help. Our one light shined on the mountainside across the lake, and hypothermia was setting in. Miraculously, someone in a house heard us and rescued us in a small boat. We had been in the icy waters for longer than forty minutes! Too long to still be alive, but we were. That's my God!

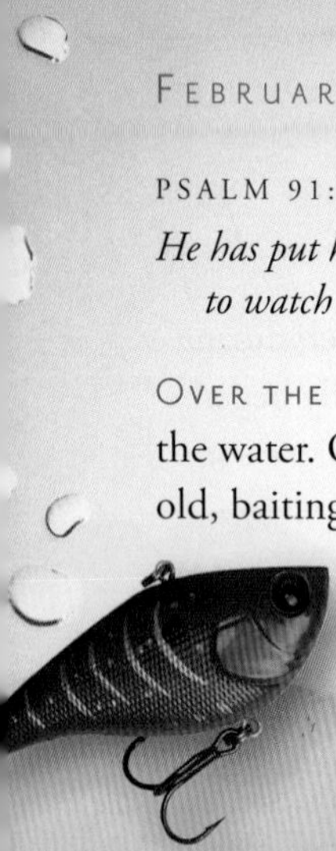

TIP

Smashing your barbs down on a Road Runner will allow you to get unsnagged easier, thus reducing the number of lures you lose.

February 12

PROVERBS 15:15

Every day is hard for those who suffer,
but a happy heart is like a continual feast.

SOME FISHERMEN seem to be happy all the time, no matter what. They seem to be having a good time and smiling under all circumstances. Is it possible that some people never have problems? Of course not.

We all experience problems, and God says every day brings trouble for some people. For the poor, this can be just having enough to eat, but for those who belong to God, life will still be abundant. Most of us have never had to worry about having enough to eat, but we still will have many days filled with trouble. Making sure we have true peace in our hearts will help overcome all our problems. When we realize what Jesus did for us, how much He loves us, and what He has prepared for us . . . it should be easy to have a joyful heart.

TIP

Bass will move to points near outside bends in creek channels in early spring.

February 13

HEBREWS 10:24

Let us think about each other and help each other to show love and do good deeds.

TOURNAMENT FISHERMEN wear their names on their shirts. This makes it easy for fishing fans to know who's who at tournaments. Without name tags, it would be tough. Even extremely recognized anglers can be confusing. For instance, folks often mistake Roland Martin and me for each other.

TIP
Use wide wobbling crankbait in cold water.

I've always thought the whole world would get along better if everyone wore a name tag. Just simply calling someone by their first name is encouragement. Spend today trying to build up those you encounter. Use every opportunity to say something nice to everyone you talk to. It won't be long until your encouragement spurs others into doing and saying positive things to and about others. With just a little effort, you're spreading love.

FEBRUARY 14

PROVERBS 20:27

The Lord looks deep inside people
and searches through their thoughts.

I LOVE TO BASS FISH at night. Even on the darkest of nights you can catch fish. I like to search out boat docks that have mercury or vapor lights on them. The added light helps casting accuracy, but the light also attracts bugs, which attract baitfish, which attract bass. One thing leads to another.

TIP

Use a red blade on your spinnerbait at night.

God not only knows and sees everything we do, but He also looks within our spirits. What does this mean? I believe it means God is well aware of our heart and our intentions even when we may be able to fool everyone else. We are laid bare before our almighty God. He knows what in our hearts will lead to which results. With this in mind, I constantly ask God to create in me a pure heart and spirit. I know that only God can make me the way He wants me to be.

February 15

JEREMIAH 17:7

The person who trusts in the L*ORD will be blessed.*

I'VE SAID MANY TIMES that if I'm not going to catch any fish, I'd rather not catch them on a spinnerbait. We all have our "confidence" baits and lures we trust to produce, even when all else fails.

Jesus is my confidence in life. I wouldn't even try to live my life without Him. I can't see why anyone would try to raise a family, grow a marriage, or build a career without a close working relationship with Jesus. Life is just too difficult to go it alone.

TIP

Use an empty parking lot to learn how to back a boat trailer.

If you have something really pressing in your life, spend a little time in God's Word and a little time talking with God. He has some remarkable solutions to whatever problems you have. He's also just waiting to help.

JOHN 15:15

"I call you friends, because I have made known to you everything I heard from my Father."

SOME OF my most exciting days as a kid were going fishing with my dad. We fished for everything—crappie, catfish, white bass, and largemouth bass. Much of what I learned about fishing came from my father.

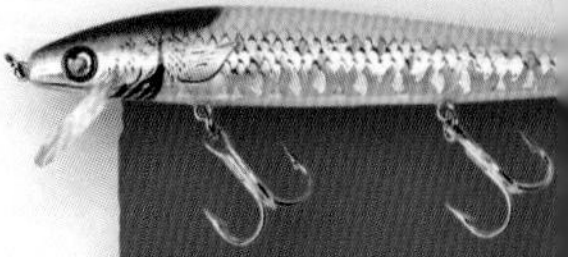

TIP

Use a trailer hook 100 percent of the time on spinnerbaits in order to learn how to use them.

Much of the way I live my life is by what my Father has told me in His Word and by His Holy Spirit. The decisions I make, the way I try to treat others, and even my attitude are determined by my heavenly Father. Folks spend millions in our society trying to learn how to improve themselves, look better, be healthier, or make more money. The list could almost go on forever. The answers are really easy; Jesus has already told us everything.

February 17

ROMANS 15:13

Then your hope will overflow by the power of the Holy Spirit.

FISHING IS MOST CERTAINLY a game of hope. For most of us, including me, we just hope we get to go fishing soon. Once we get on the water, we have an abundance of hope resting on every cast. Without hope, we might as well stay home.

Without God, we have no hope for eternity. God has instilled in us the knowledge and desire for eternal life. He has also provided us with the way to eternal life with Him. This way is Jesus. Jesus died for our sins so we could have eternal life with Him in heaven. This is a Christian's hope, and life would be meaningless without it. Our life would simply be living day-by-day, fearing death. With Jesus, we are assured of eternal life with God.

TIP

Always carry Dip-N-Dye or marker pens to add color to your lures.

NEHEMIAH 8:10

Don't be sad, because the joy of the LORD will make you strong.

MY WIFE, CHRIS, has always said that the great thing about fishing is you don't have to be strong or tall or fast or especially gifted to fish. I have fished with many people who have significant physical handicaps. We still had a lot of fun and caught fish.

Nehemiah told the people the joy of the Lord—not their physical abilities—was their strength. Knowing Jesus on a personal basis produces a joy that overcomes anything this world can throw at us. It allows us to be strong no matter how serious or how dejected we might otherwise become. This joy is difficult for a non-Christian to understand, but it overflows in one who knows Jesus.

TIP

Have your outboard tuned in early spring to save gas money every fishing trip.

FEBRUARY 19

PROVERBS 3:9

Honor the L*ORD with your wealth*
and the first fruits from all your crops.

DARREL ROBERTSON from Oklahoma won the first really giant purse in bass fishing . . . over $600,000 in the Ranger Millennium Tournament in 1999. Still today, this is one of the biggest payouts ever. Darrel used $100,000 of that money to build a new activity center for his church.

TIP

Throw at any movement on the water.

To a real believer, giving to the Lord is not an option; it's an honor. Tithes and offerings are not something you do if you can afford it. Tithes and offerings are something you do *before* you spend the rest of your money. I believe if we do not tithe, we don't allow God to pour out His blessing on us. We actually cheat ourselves out of something God intended us to have.

FEBRUARY 20

JOHN 16:33

"In this world you will have trouble, but be brave! I have defeated the world."

HOW WE HANDLE adversity is one of the great traits of a champion fisherman. No matter how good you get, how much knowledge, how great your ability . . . trials will come, and they generally will come often. At times, this world is going to throw more problems at us than we think we can bear. This is because Satan is ruler of this world, and that's the business Satan is about—causing problems for everyone and especially believers in Jesus. Can a Christian handle adversity better than a nonbeliever? Absolutely!

We live by faith that Jesus has overcome the world and that He is able to see us through whatever Satan puts on our plate. We never have to face these tribulations alone.

TIP

Drag your fishing line without a lure behind the boat to remove line twist.

FEBRUARY 21

PSALM 35:9

Then I will rejoice in the LORD;
I will be happy when he saves me.

MANY TOURNAMENT WINNERS today stand on the stage and thank God for their victories. Some even give Jesus the credit and glory for the win. I believe winning does indeed give a Christian an opportunity to witness and praise God. The champion is center stage. Everyone is hanging on every word. But perhaps just as important is how we react and act when we suffer defeat. Because no matter who you are, someone is always watching and listening.

Are we being Christlike in defeat, or are we complaining, making excuses, and being envious of the winner? When Jesus was crucified, Satan thought he had won. But the victory belonged to Jesus, and because of His victory we, too, can rejoice in victory every day and under all circumstances.

TIP

When you use live bait, a kale bend or circle type bend hook will help prevent bass from swallowing your hook.

February 22

JOB 23:10

God knows the way that I take,
and when he has tested me, I will come out like gold.

A Global Positioning System (GPS) is now a staple for any serious fisherman. We all have spots, or waypoints, marked on our GPS units, and we can go directly to those spots no matter how far away they are. Even in dense fog, we can locate an exact spot. My Humminbird 1198 is in full color and even has an unbelievable sonar system built into the unit. It's really a high-tech marvel.

God's Positioning System is even more remarkable. Not only does He know where He's going, but He also knows where each of us is going. He knows all of us, even what we're thinking. Sometimes our lives seem to be in a dense fog, and we get into situations where we can't see. Don't worry. Don't panic. God's Positioning System knows right where we are. Ask Him and He will lead you safely out of the fog.

TIP

When fishing a lying down log, keep your boat a little farther away than usual.

JAMES 4:14

But you do not know what will happen tomorrow! Your life is like a mist. You can see it for a short time, but then it goes away.

ONE OF MY most frightening moments as a teenager on Lake Tenkiller happened on a foggy morning as I motored my fourteen-foot aluminum boat through the fog to run a trotline. I knew the lake like I knew my own bedroom. Fog was no problem. I ran wide open toward a point where the line was tied. When I was halfway to the point, a rock bank suddenly appeared within a few feet of my bow. I turned the motor hard, but beached the boat fifteen to twenty feet up on the bank.

TIP

Almost every strike on a jig will come on the fall.

I was unhurt, but scared silly. Fortunately, I only had a twenty-horsepower Mercury. I had no idea where I was. Then the fog went away, and I was no longer lost. God says our life will also go quickly, and we must be ready for eternity.

1 PETER 2:1–2

So then rid yourselves of all evil, lying, hypocrisy, jealousy, and evil speech. As newborn babies want milk, you should want the pure and simple teaching.

DECEIT IS REALLY the basis for all fishing done with an artificial lure. We're constantly trying to deceive the fish and make them believe our lure is really something very good to eat.

Unfortunately, a lot of life is handled the same way. So much of business, advertising, and personal behavior is shrouded in deceit. Many people, including Christians, use deceit as a normal means of behavior. This may work in the short-term, but according to God's Word failure is inevitable. When you pray today, instead of asking God for the usual things you want, ask God to take away any deceit, hypocrisy, or backstabbing you may have in your life.

TIP

Bass eat crawdads when their pinchers are tucked, not when they are open in a defensive position.

February 25

PSALM 23:4

Even if I walk through a very dark valley, I will not be afraid, because you are with me.

My dad and my two uncles, Gene and John, would fish the Ouachita River in Arkansas for catfish in July and August. The hot summer months were best because the river was low and mostly dry, and the channel cats would concentrate in deeper holes. We would walk for miles up and down the river searching out these holes. Being impatient, I would always be down the river ahead of the rest. What panic I would feel when I would realize I was all alone and had left my dad and uncles behind. What great relief when I would finally see them coming.

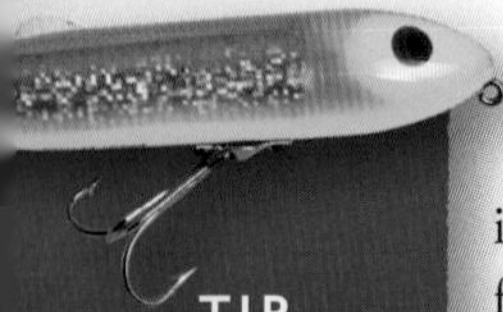

TIP

Fire Tiger is the bestselling crankbait color in the country.

Jesus has promised that we need never be afraid. When everyone has deserted us, Jesus is always there.

FEBRUARY 26

ROMANS 12:6

We all have different gifts, each of which came because of the grace God gave us.

A YOUNG MAN about nine or ten years old asked me if I had been a professional fisherman since I was a kid. I told him no, but that I had loved fishing since I was old enough to walk. There was no such thing as pro fishermen until many years after I graduated from college. Even then, though, God knew there would be pros, and He had given me and others the ability to be professional bass fishermen.

Realize this: whatever ability or talent you have has come from God. He has given you these abilities to use for His glory. Use them for that purpose today.

TIP

Windy banks on the north and east shorelines warm up faster early in the year.

February 27

ISAIAH 41:10

Don't worry, because I am with you.

When my grandson Jeremy was about four years old, he decided to take his dog and do a little exploring at a pond near his house. The pond was big and deep, especially for a four-year-old who didn't bother asking or telling anyone about his trip. Much like Jesus' parents when they discovered Him missing, my daughter, Sherri, panicked and had everyone else in a panic with her. She called Chris and me at a tournament, and we were also concerned. A frantic hour or so later, Jeremy and his Labrador retriever showed up safe. Was he afraid? Of course not. He had his dog, and although he didn't understand it at the time, his God was with him. Such is God's care over His children and their children.

TIP

Keep a lookout for white and blue herons. Fish the same spots where they are feeding.

PSALM 84:11

He does not hold back anything good
from those whose lives are innocent.

IF ONLY *I could catch some more bass . . . If only I could get that big bite . . . If only I could win a tournament . . . If only I could get a new sponsor . . . If only I could turn pro . . .* Life is full of "if onlys."

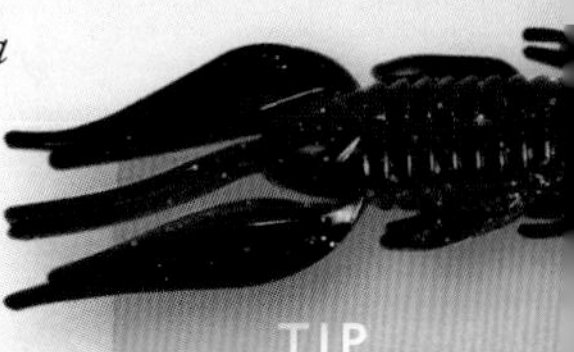

TIP

Work the edges of tree lines immediately after a bass spawn.

For a Christian, God has the answer for our "if onlys." Not just some of the "if onlys," but all of them. The secret is simply to do what is right and let God deliver . . . and He will. He won't necessarily deliver everything we desire, because not everything we want is a good thing. God knows the end results, and He has the power to control everything for our good. Trust God to do what's best.

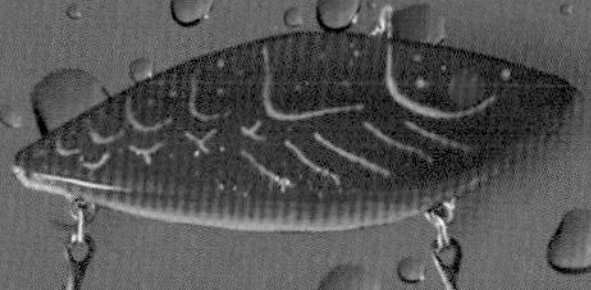

March

JOHN 3:16

"God loved the world so much that he gave his one and only Son so that whoever believes in him may not be lost, but have eternal life."

This is the front-row verse to most Americans. We see the guy with the funny hair hold John 3:16 posters up at many sporting events. I've even seen him at the Bassmaster Classic. But it's also the salvation verse. The entire gospel of how to be saved is right there. God loved, He gave, we believe, and we have eternal life. We're saved because God loved us. He gave His Son to pay for our sin.

When we say we believe, that means more than simply believing there is a God or there is a Jesus. The word *believe* also means trust, among other things. We trust in Him, and we receive life eternal with God. That's how simple the gospel actually is. Wow!

TIP

With most crankbaits, you can move to one size larger treble hooks.

PROVERBS 14:23

Those who work hard make a profit,
but those who only talk will be poor.

IN ORDER to really learn how to catch fish, we must put a lot of work into the game. It is true that many people have a lot of fun just being out on the water, whether they catch a fish or not. But most of us work hard at fishing because of the pleasure and excitement we get when we actually get a fish on the end of our line.

God has instilled in each of us this desire to work hard in order to be rewarded at the end of our labor. In fishing, I believe that the harder I work, the luckier I get. The one thing God does not require us to work for is our salvation. This is God's free gift to us and requires only believing on our part.

TIP

White bass, hybrids, and stripers will move to the upper ends of rivers and creeks in early spring.

March 3

JOHN 11:26

"Everyone who lives and believes in me shall never die."

THE FIRST TIME I remember anything being given to me because of my fishing happened in the late 1960s at a tournament on Sam Rayburn Lake in Texas. John Fox of the *American Angler Television Show* gave me a handful of Mister Twister worms. These were the first plastic worms with a curly tail. I caught a lot of fish on those worms, and so did all my buddies. I told everyone how great they were.

TIP

A spin tail bait like a Little George works great in rivers for all species.

God has given us the greatest gifts we can ever receive—eternal life and a joy and hope for everyday living that can never fade away. Yet so many of us Christians don't share this gift with our buddies. Today, share with a friend what God is doing in your life. What a great tip that will be.

March 4

PSALM 119:2

Happy are those who keep his rules.

ARE ALL FISHERMEN LIARS, or do all liars fish? It is amazing that very few fishermen can tell a fish story without stretching the truth. I've asked hundreds of little kids to show me how big their biggest fish was, and invariably they will stretch their hands wide apart.

But sticking to the true real truth about life is a gift from God. God laid down laws that He intends for us to obey. These laws are for our own good and were given to create happiness in our life. When we bend the laws, we will always create situations that deprive us of our happiness. Sure, we may get away with doing something wrong when no one is looking, but ultimately, we'll never be happy with the results.

TIP

Learn to work a few lures really well.

March 5

JOHN 13:34

"You must love each other as I have loved you."

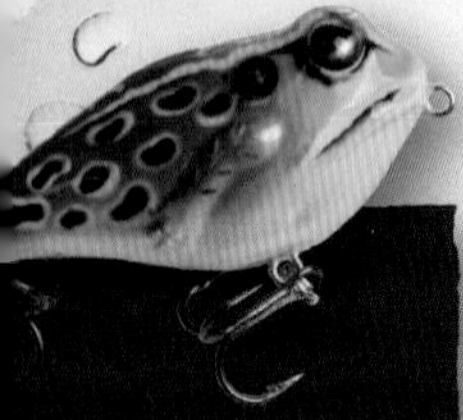

TIP

Use a bobber above a Road Runner to catch crappie over shallow brush piles.

Fishing creates long-lasting relationships. Like so many people, some of my best friends are my fishing buddies. One of my wife's closest friends ever was Ricky Green's wife, Bettye, who has passed away. I remember Chris sitting and holding her all night a few days just before she died. You could easily see the love Chris had developed for Bettye over the years of our fishing together.

Jesus tells us the proof that we love Him is that we love one another. This love really needs to surpass any of the other feelings that come into our relationships. When another Christian does you wrong, disappoints you, or treats you badly, your response should simply be to love him or her as Jesus loves you.

March 6

PROVERBS 17:6

Old people are proud of their grandchildren,
and children are proud of their parents.

PROBABLY THE BEST way to get your kids and grandkids into fishing is to take them perch or bluegill fishing. You can catch bluegill just about anywhere you can find water. Teach them how to tie on a hook, pinch on a split shot, and attach a bobber. Learning to cast, concentrating on the bobber, setting the hook, and handling the fish are just a few of the important lessons.

TIP

Heavy spoons jigged vertically around standing timber will produce cold-water bass.

God created the family, and then He created fishing as another means of holding families together. Plan some time in your schedule in the next couple of weeks to take your kids or grandkids perch fishing. Resist all the other more sought-after species. Your family is well worth the trip!

March 7

ROMANS 14:19

So let us try to do what makes peace and helps one another.

AWHILE BACK, I fished with a thirteen-year-old girl, Tamara, who had won a fishin' trip with me. She's a beautiful young lady who loves the outdoors and loves to fish. That day, however, she put her spinnerbait in the trees many times throughout the day. I kidded her, singing "George, George, George of the jungle . . . watch out for that tree." Mostly though, I encouraged her and congratulated her on every good cast. (And there were many!) She also caught several good bass.

TIP

A prop on a topwater emulates extremely small baitfish on the surface.

We all make mistakes. We all mess up. God forgives our mistakes and continually encourages us to do better. We need to do the same with one another.

March 8

ECCLESIASTES 11:1

Invest what you have,
because after a while you will get a return.

AT MY AGE, I'm often asked why I continue to fish national bass tournaments. They take a lot of time and are a tremendous mental and physical strain on my body, not to mention the enormous amount of travel. Of course, I still enjoy the tournaments and the time with my friends. And the tournaments are profitable! The most important reason is that I want to give back to the game that has given so much to me. But, just like giving to God, I can't outgive this game. I've often tried to outgive God, but He always gives back more. This is one of God's greatest principles. Try it for yourself.

TIP

Use the lowest speed on your trolling motor that you can get by with.

MARCH 9

GALATIANS 6:9

We must not become tired of doing good.

CASTING ACCURACY is really an important part of bass fishing. Just a 5 percent or 10 percent improvement can make a difference in a fisherman's catch. The only way I know to become good is to use good technique and practice a lot. Sometimes it's frustrating to practice hard and seemingly see no improvement, but trust me: practice will make you better.

TIP
Use a white buzzbait on warm, rainy, spring days.

In life, we struggle sometimes with trying to do what's right and good without anybody noticing or caring. We work hard, we help, we give, we love, and we don't receive much in return. God says to never get tired. God's watching, and He knows about even the good thoughts we have. Go out and do something good today.

MARCH 10

EPHESIANS 4:29

When you talk, do not say harmful things.

I LOVE TO VISIT with the people I'm fishing with when I am just fishing for fun. Some of my best days fishing have been with my very good friend Joe Hall, owner of Blakemore Road Runners. We talk about everything from our beautiful wives to politics to business. Sometimes I'm talking about one thing while Joe is talking about something entirely different. Amazingly, we still catch fish.

TIP

When floating a stream, don't try to cover too much territory in a day. Take your time.

God gave us the ability to communicate so we can be helpful to one another. One of my most frequent prayers is "Please, God, don't let me say anything bad about anybody." I guess if I would just concentrate on saying something good, nothing bad could come out.

March 11

2 TIMOTHY 4:2

Encourage them with great patience and careful teaching.

TIP

A suspended crankbait will stay in the strike zone longer, yielding more fish in cold water.

Kids Day on Lake Tenkiller is always the first Saturday in June. We allow the first five hundred kids who sign up to attend. But get this: we have more than one hundred volunteers. These volunteers range from teenagers (some who attended Kids Day earlier in their lives) to guys and gals over seventy years old. It's a pure joy to watch them patiently teach and encourage those young kids learning to fish. Believe me, not all of those five hundred kids are easy to be patient with.

Pause for a moment or two today and think of someone who was encouraging as he or she patiently taught you something. When you come up with a couple of names, now would be a great time to thank them. By the way, don't forget your mom or dad.

March 12

JOHN 15:19

"I have chosen you out of the world."

Don Butler won the 1972 Bassmaster Classic with a bait called an SOB (Small Okiebug). This is a small crankbait. Many times, early in the year, a smaller bait will produce a lot of fish. For one thing, most fishermen in the tournament were fishing larger spinnerbaits trying to catch large spawning females. Also, the fish were really getting a lot of pressure and seeing a lot of baits. Fishing with something different was the key to success in that tournament.

TIP

Small blades allow for more accurate casting.

God has called us out of the world to be different. We are to be more loving, more caring, more joyful, more generous, and more forgiving than non-Christians. Some days we fail, but God is continually working to make our difference shine.

March 13

ACTS 5:29

We must obey God, not human authority!

BASS, CRAPPIE, and most freshwater game fish spawn in the spring and early summer. Many are very predictable because of this annual springtime event that repopulates the waters. We know to fish back in protected pockets and coves. We look for hard bottoms and gentle sloping banks, pea gravel, or sand if we can find it. These spawning fish are following God's laws in order to reproduce and keep their species going. They have no other law to obey; only God's.

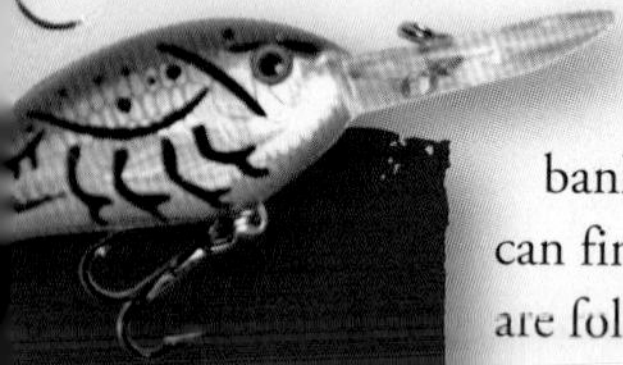

TIP

Look for spawning bass behind boat docks and around walkways.

Man's law in our country is becoming increasingly in conflict with what God has told us to do. As time goes by, this will become more and more prevalent. In order to prevail, as Christians, we must still obey God's Word.

March 14

PSALM 103:2

Praise the L*ORD*
and do not forget all his kindnesses.

ALMOST ALL FISHERMEN highly anticipate early spring fishing, but we hardly ever anticipate or remember that most early springs are dominated by high winds. Oh, do we hate fishing in the wind! But the spring wind really is our friend and very beneficial for catching fish. It pushes the warm surface water up on the shorelines (usually the north and eastern shorelines) and warms the water. This brings in the baitfish and the bass that create great fishing. The same wind we hate becomes a blessing.

God is working every day in each Christian's life to make all things beneficial. This includes problems, people, and circumstances. Never lose sight of God's blessing in all situations.

TIP

Pay very close attention to your water temp gauge in the spring.

March 15

DEUTERONOMY 6:7

Teach [the LORD's commands] to your children.

CHRIS AND I started our two kids, Jamie and Sherri, working in the family business when they were nine or ten years old. We wanted them to learn the kind of effort and work ethic necessary to be successful. We wanted them to learn integrity in business and how to deal with people. We also gave them important jobs to do.

God demands that we teach our kids about Him. We should do this daily. My God is an everyday God, not just a Sunday God. What you teach doesn't have to be some big theological lesson. It can be as simple as talking about some small blessing God gave you that day. What's important is to lead your kids into a working relationship with Jesus.

TIP

A black/chartreuse lizard will produce well during spawning season.

March 16

MATTHEW 6:6

"When you pray, you should go into your room and close the door and pray to your Father."

A FEW YEARS AGO, I spent a couple of days fishing with my close friend Ray Scott, founder of BASS. We spent one evening sitting in his living room until the wee hours of the morning. We were visiting about our many years together, as bass fishing grew from nothing to where it is today. It was a wonderful time as we remembered story after story.

God wants this type of intimate conversations with His children. Public prayer is one thing, but personal prayer is *mano de mano* with the Creator of the universe. How awesome it is that the almighty God actually wants to be involved in this conversation!

TIP

A turtle in the water indicates some underwater brush is nearby.

MARCH 17

JOHN 6:43

"Stop complaining to each other."

ANYONE WHO has taken kids on a fishing trip understands that they will always fuss with each other. Brothers are bad, but put a brother and sister in the same boat and get ready for some fireworks. This is standard behavior for kids, but unfortunately some carry this disposition throughout their lives. For a Christian, this is totally unacceptable behavior to God.

When God saves us, He places His Holy Spirit in us. The Holy Spirit produces much fruit—including joy—and none of this holy fruit includes grumbling. If you're saved, act like it!

TIP

Marabou jigs have more action in cold water than plastic or rubber.

MARCH 18

PHILIPPIANS 4:6

Do not worry about anything, but pray and ask God for everything you need, always giving thanks.

EARLY SPRING is without a doubt the very best time to catch real lunker bass. Bass come out of the winter season where they have been almost dormant like couch potatoes. They get big and fat. Lunker females bulge with eggs. A fisherman's biggest concern during the spring is getting enough time off to go fishing, but actually catching bass is nothing to worry about during this wonderful time of the year.

Having a close relationship with Jesus allows us the freedom to not worry about anything at any time of the year. God has promised to take care of our needs. He has given us the guarantee of eternal life with Him and an abundant life here on Earth.

TIP

Match your jig colors to the available baitfish.

March 19

PROVERBS 22:4

Respecting the LORD *and not being proud*
will bring you wealth, honor, and life.

I'VE BEEN very fortunate to fish with many great fishermen. These include George W. Bush, Davey Allison, Ken Griffey Jr., Toby Keith, Terry Bradshaw, Barry Switzer, and many, many other well-known folks. All of these guys have a lot to be proud of, but I've noted a common thread among them all: they are all very humble. They are quick to give a lot of credit to others and slow to brag on themselves.

TIP
Switch to a jointed jerkbait if you are missing fish on regular jerkbait.

God tells us that humility is a definite route to success. Humbling ourselves *toward* God is good, but humbling yourself *before* God is what He desires. Whatever your achievement, remember the God who gave you that success.

March 20

MARK 5:36

"Don't be afraid; just believe."

WOMEN HAVE been a big part of my fishing life. Chris and I spent a lot of our early dates in a fishing boat, and, yes, most of the time we were actually fishing. We pretty much raised our daughter Sherri in a bass boat. Now, some of my best days are teaching my granddaughter, Jordyn, to fish. But even today, it is still unusual to see two women fishing in a bass boat. Chris and Sherri have never been afraid to go fishing alone, because they know what they're doing under just about any circumstance. They trust their knowledge.

TIP

Teach all members of your family, including the kids, how to operate your boat.

God wants us to believe Him and not be afraid no matter what. This trust comes from absolutely knowing that you belong to Him and that He will never forsake you.

March 21

JAMES 5:13

Anyone who is having troubles should pray.

LIGHTNING STRIKES CAN be one of the most frightening things to happen out on the water. In most lakes, your boat is the tallest thing around and is a sure target for lightning. Some of the hottest storms Chris and I have ever encountered have been on East Texas lakes such as Rayburn, Toledo Bend, and Lake Fork. Your best bet when lightning comes where you're fishing is either to get under a bridge or go to the bank and find cover. Obviously, a lightning storm is one of those good times to pray.

TIP

A subtle rattle in a crankbait is sometimes better in clear water.

For a lot of believers, trouble is the only time they let God work in their lives. God will be there to carry us through our storms, but if we let Him walk with us every day, He will keep us out of most trouble.

March 22

2 THESSALONIANS 3:3

But the Lord is faithful and will give you strength and will protect you from the Evil One.

Bass move to really heavy cover when the water rises in the spring. A rule of thumb is the heavier the cover, the bigger the bass. My weapon to get to these giant females is a jig. One little trick is to flare the weed guard on your jig. This keeps you from getting hung up so easily, but it also displaces the stiffness of the weed guard to allow for an easier hook set.

Just like those bass respond when the water rises, Christians have their own defense when the devil attacks—the armor of God. When we claim the power He gives us through His Word, His Spirit, His righteousness, and His peace, we can stand against Satan's schemes. We claim that power through prayer. So when Satan attacks, pray! You will be amazed at how quickly God will come to help.

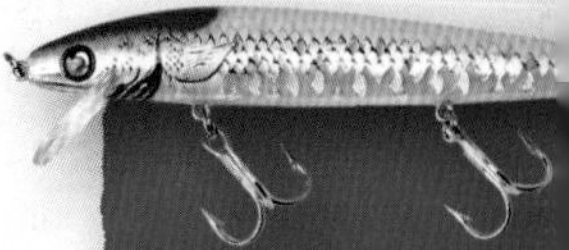

TIP

A sinking worm with a hook slot like a Yum Dinger provides easier hook sets.

March 23

JEREMIAH 31:33

I will put my teachings in their minds
and write them on their hearts.

PAT TURNER, who shoots camera and runs our production company, has never spent a great deal of time fishing. Sure, he gets to fish for a couple of hours after we finish taping a television show, but most of the time he's just watching through that camera. However, he's also learning and observing, and over the last ten years, he has become one of the most knowledgeable fishermen in the country. Years of taping and editing *Jimmy Houston Outdoors* have filled his mind with knowledge about this game.

TIP
Use the lightest slip sinker as you can comfortably fish.

For similar reasons, it's so important for a person to have a daily working relationship with Jesus. This includes prayer, Bible reading, and fellowship with God's people. Try it, and before long you'll become far more knowledgeable and will understand what God desires in every circumstance.

March 24

PSALM 119:80

Let me obey your demands perfectly
so I will not be ashamed.

I LOVE TO SLOW ROLL a Booyah spinnerbait over submerged grass in the early spring. That is where a lot of the big female bass are staging before going shallow to spawn. Try to learn to just barely tick the top of the grass with your bait. Keeping your spinnerbait at just the right depth is the key to catching big strings of big bass, just as keeping God's laws is the key to everything we do in life.

Integrity is not something we are born with. In fact, we were born with just the opposite . . . *sin*. No matter what, we must learn to not cut corners when we get in a bind. When a situation arises, ask God to help you rely on His principles. Grow your integrity.

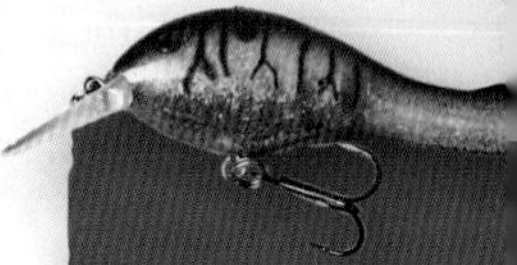

TIP

Don't be afraid to mix and match some wild colors of spinnerbaits, such as a bubblegum (hot pink) head with a chartreuse skirt.

MARCH 25

1 JOHN 2:6

Whoever says that he lives in God must live as Jesus lived.

MOST OF US have our ideas and techniques about fishin' developed by the folks we fish with. My skills about trotlining for catfish were learned from my dad and uncles. My kids and grandkids love to fish a spinnerbait. (I wonder where that came from!)

TIP

Bass become very active on warm, sunny afternoons in the early spring.

All of us are affected greatly by the people we respect and look up to, so shouldn't what we say about how to live be directed by the greatest Person who ever walked this earth? Jesus is that Person, and His life was lived in perfection. Today, ask God to give you the mindset of Jesus. Pause in every situation and relationship, and give God a chance to let you react like Jesus. Just a two-second pause is all God needs to work miracles if you're serious about letting Him.

MARCH 26

JOB 1:22

In all this Job did not sin or blame God.

EVERY FISHING TRIP has its challenges, but if you want even more challenges, jump into a few bass tournaments and see what real fishing troubles are all about.

Sometimes it seems that just getting by day by day is a terrific struggle, but keep in mind that struggles have a benefit. We learn much more at the bottom than we do at the top of the heap. It's good to look at challenges as great opportunities to learn and build character. God will actually use these hardships to build you as a Christian.

We all know Job as the king of trouble and hardship. When we read about Job the first time, it's almost impossible not to cry for the guy. When we finish the story, we see what God can make out of our troubles. What an awesome God!

TIP

Don't overlook shallow stumps as places for bass to spawn.

March 27

PHILIPPIANS 4:4

Be full of joy in the Lord always, I will say again, be full of joy.

IT'S REALLY EASY for me to have fun fishing. It's so easy, I can have a lot of fun even when the fish aren't biting. But what about enjoying the things that we don't like? What about having fun during the difficult times? Can we really rejoice in the Lord always? You bet we can! To me, joy is a purposeful attitude that I try to put on every day. I'm resolved to make it a great day no matter what. Do I succeed every day? No! Do I have bad days? Of course! But I am sure of this . . . anyone can develop this quality of joy. Get into the habit every day of asking God to help you do it. Now go out and have a fun day.

TIP

On your home lake, make sure you fish at least one new spot every day.

EPHESIANS 2:10

God has made us what we are. In Christ Jesus, God made us to do good works.

THE AREA around Ithaca and Corning, New York, has some of the best lakes in the country. They are deep and clear with smallmouth, largemouth, lake trout, northern pike, and many other species of fish. These are natural lakes, not dammed-up rivers and creeks. God created these lakes for our benefit. He also created us to help one another.

We are born again in Christ, and God expects us to do good to one another. Too much of the time, we become self-centered and are only concerned about ourselves. We live as if we are the only people who count. We become a "me" generation! If you claim Christ, spend today doing good works that benefit others.

TIP

Big fish get under dead water hyacinths in the early spring.

March 29

1 CORINTHIANS 10:23

"We are allowed to do all things," but not all things are good for us to do.

EVER WONDER why you catch so many small bass and not too many big ones? Sure, there are more little ones than lunkers, and a lot of bass get eaten before they have many birthdays, some by bigger bass. The main reason is those older bass are a whole lot wiser. After they've been caught, kissed, and released a time or two, they're pretty hard to fool! Especially if they are caught by a lousy kisser.

We're much like those small bass during our high school and college years. We're out on our own just enough to have the chance to try anything, and some of us do. Like those small bass, our decisions can sometimes cost us dearly. It's critical to live close to God during those years and then maintain that closeness throughout our lives.

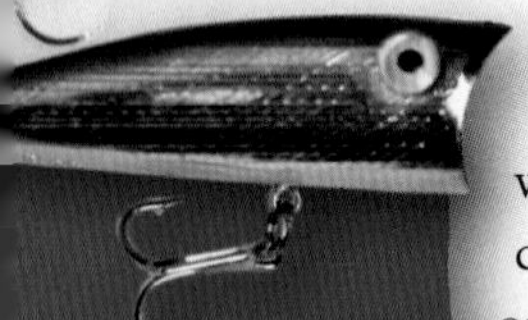

TIP

Try a crawdad color crankbait on chunk rock banks in late March.

March 30

PSALM 37:7

Wait and trust the Lord.

I won a Bass-n-Race tournament at Disney World in Orlando while teamed up with Bobby Allison, the great NASCAR legend. Bobby was a terrific fisherman, especially with plastic worms, which is what we caught our fish with midway through that tournament morning. Early that day they were tearing up a Rebel Pop-R, but they were usually missing the bait on the first strike and not getting hooked until the second or third bite. These were dynamite blowups. When the bass struck, Bobby set the hook. He made up for it later with worms, and we caught our limit. We won the tournament and caught big bass.

TIP

The longer you pause a jerkbait, the more strikes you generally get.

We all get impatient with God at times. When you know what a powerful God He is, you come to expect miracles from Him all the time. But be patient; it's His timetable.

March 31

NEHEMIAH 2:20

The God of heaven will give us success.

About the easiest way to catch any species of fish is with live bait. The really successful guides in Florida use live bait to produce those giant Florida bass for their clients. Live bait is so effective, it's not even legal in bass tournaments.

The way to success with your family, your job, or anything else is with the Living God. He has been at the core of everything good we have done. Whatever success we've had in our family, fishing, or business has come from God. Yes, there have been many struggles and trials, but through my darkest moments, God was not walking with me—He was carrying me. What a blessing to live in God's arms!

TIP

Try a small slip sinker like a Yum Dinger on a sinking worm.

April

April 1

2 THESSALONIANS 2:16

God loved us, and through his grace he gave us a good hope and encouragement that continues forever.

Fishing a Zara Spook topwater bait is a tiring but productive method of fishing. Sometimes it is critical to work the bait just at the right pace to trigger a strike. Years ago when I was teaching my daughter, Sherri, to fish a Zara Spook, she figured out a way to work the bait with a consistent "walk." She would sing "Jesus Loves Me" and make the bait "walk" back to the boat to the rhythm of that classic children's song. Working the bait to the words of that song not only helps you work the bait at the right pace, but it reminds you of that wonderful truth—"Jesus loves me, this I know!"

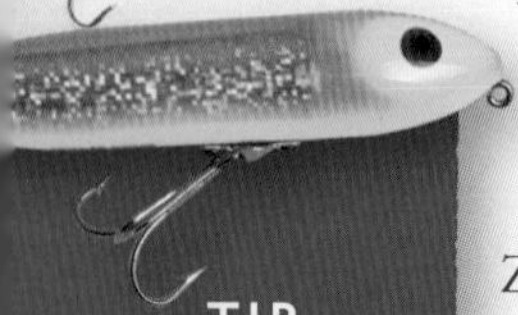

TIP

When fishing a topwater, let the bait lie still a few seconds before working it back to the boat.

April 2

PHILIPPIANS 4:13

*I can do all things through Christ,
because he gives me strength.*

THE FIRST FIVE MONTHS of the year are killers for me. I do more than fifty personal appearances all over the country, fish four or five tournaments, and tape several fishing and hunting shows for NBC Sports, My Family TV, America One Network, Access Media Group, and The Texas Channel. Sleep is at a premium. Many nights we get to bed around midnight or later only to get back up around four or five to start all over again. This takes a huge toll on a person's mind and body. Most of my close friends are amazed that what we do is even humanly possible. Well, it's not! God enables me to keep this kind of schedule. He gives me strength for my benefit and to serve Him. I find that the more I serve Him daily, the more strength He gives me—both mentally and physically.

TIP

Believe you're going to get a bite on every cast.

April 3

ROMANS 12:2

Be changed within by a new way of thinking.

If, like me, you've fished for more years than most other people have lived, you've gained a lot of knowledge and skill about this fishin' game. But this vast amount of experience and know-how can be a trap. We can't keep up if we're not continually learning new techniques and skills both on and off the water.

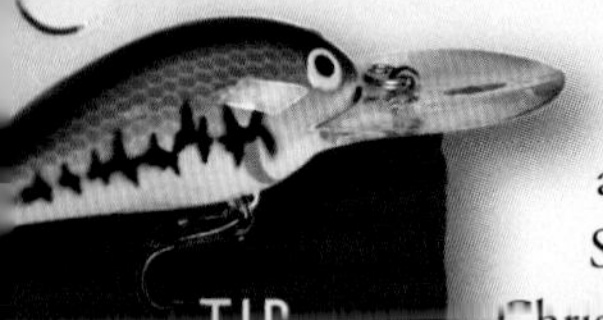

TIP

Search out clay or mud banks with visible crawdad holes.

Similarly, many of us have been Christians for a long, long time. Some of us are growing daily, while others of us are as stagnant as a half-dry creek bed in August. Gradually we become like the rest of the world, living our lives no differently than non-Christians are. It's really important to read God's Word and talk to Him every day. This allows God to continually transform us into the kind of people He wants us to be.

April 4

PROVERBS 11:24

Some people give much but get back even more.

FISHERMEN GET on a roll sometimes during a day or a few weeks or even for a few months. As Jerry Reed put it in a song: "When you're hot, you're hot!" Your decision-making is good, your casting is superb, you're even luckier. When this happens, relish the moment.

TIP

A small buzzbait works well in dead calm water.

One way to stay on a roll is by giving freely—giving your money, your time, your skills, your talents. Amazingly, your loving God has promised that the more you give, the more you will gain. I've tested this promise over and over, and it's never failed.

Do you want more money? Tithe.

Do you want to be a better fisherman? Give your knowledge and skills to a kid or someone just learning to fish.

Give more, gain more!

April 5

LEVITICUS 19:18

Love your neighbor as you love yourself.

BEFORE THE DAYS of catch and release, Chris and I had a way to be very popular with our friends and neighbors. We almost always caught more fish than we could eat, and we pretty much kept everyone we knew supplied in fish. Most of the time, we would fillet and bag the fish for them. (Chris can really fillet fish!)

TIP
Check the grease in your trailer bearings every three or four months.

Too often today, many folks don't even know their neighbors, let alone love them. We tend more and more to isolate ourselves from those around us. God never intended this. We help those we love. We encourage and build up those we love. We feed and protect. This is God's will and His design. Reach out and get to know and love a neighbor today, whether at home or at work. God just might make sure that neighbor loves you back.

MARK 9:37

"Whoever accepts a child like this in my name accepts me."

THERE'S A FISHIN' CLUB near Auburn, New York, that has been doing a kids fishin' day for fifty-eight years. *Fifty-eight years!* That's incredible! They've grown over the years, and now many grandfathers and even great-grandfathers who attended as youngsters are helping reach the children. These fishin' days go back four generations. What a great legacy of love those men and women are passing on year after year!

TIP

Teach your child to tie a really good knot.

Jesus welcomed the little children. Their minds, hearts, and souls are shaped by God Himself and not yet tainted by the world—that's why we're told to have the faith of a child. Why were the children so important to Jesus, and why should they be so important to us? Because they soon will grow up into moms and dads and grandmas and granddads. Such will inherit the kingdom of God.

APRIL 7

GALATIANS 5:22–23

The Spirit produces the fruit of love, joy, peace, patience, kindness, goodness, faithfulness, gentleness, self-control.

ALL THE BASS PRO SHOPS have huge fish tanks with all kinds of fish. We also have a large tank in our Jimmy Houston Outdoors Store on Lake Tenkiller. It's fascinating just to sit and watch those fish. It doesn't take long to realize that fish, just like people, have their own personalities and behaviors.

TIP

Always charge all your boat batteries after every use.

I've often wondered why some Christians who possess God's Spirit don't very often exhibit the fruit of that Spirit. I wonder why we're not happy all of the time. Maybe it's because we're so concerned about our own little wants and needs that the Spirit can't blossom. Maybe Satan is attacking our attitudes to keep us from the Spirit's fruit. Whatever the reason, I am going to reach up and grab some of that fruit today.

APRIL 8

JOSHUA 1:9

Don't be afraid, because the LORD your God will be with you everywhere you go.

MY FIRST ATTEMPT at fishing a tournament in California was Lake Oroville. I borrowed a boat from the local Ranger dealer after flying to the tournament, and then I headed to the lake for the three days of official practice. Oroville was so clear, you could read heads or tails on a dime twenty feet deep. I practiced two days without a bite. On the last day of practice, I traveled as far up the river as I could go and began fishing white Road Runners with a half of a pork strip trailer. Throwing at cracks in steep bluffs, we started catching bass—lots of bass. During competition I caught more than sixty bass every day, and won the tournament by two ounces.

If you belong to Christ, take heart and be persistent; He is right there even when you seem to be failing.

TIP

In the South, most bass will spawn under the March or April full moon.

April 9

PROVERBS 29:11

Foolish people lose their tempers,
but wise people control theirs.

SUBMERGED STUMPS are pretty much always a great place to find a bass. The very best stumps will be the ones you can just barely see. They're a little bit deeper, and mostly they get overlooked by other fishermen. Generally the best technique is to bump the stump with a spinnerbait. I like Vibra-FLX spinnerbaits because they're almost impossible to hang up. Depth control and direction are finesse techniques that need to be learned.

TIP

Buy good fishing line. The cheap stuff is a heartache waiting to happen.

God says it's wise to have another kind of depth control—self-control. The old trick of counting to ten before you speak or react is still as good as gold. If we will just pause for a moment when we are offended or get upset, we'll give God's Spirit the chance to take control so we stay calm and cool.

April 10

JAMES 1:3

You know that these troubles test your faith, and this will give you patience.

LEARNING TO CAST a casting reel can try anyone's patience. For most, it takes a lot of backlashes and horrible casts before you even begin to learn. For me, it was almost impossible. The trick is to open the reel up and keep constant contact on the spool throughout the throws. It may take time, but you can learn.

TIP

As the water warms, you can increase your speed of retrieve.

Daily trials constantly try our faith in Jesus and His ability to handle our problems. We're not alone. Jesus often admonished His closest disciples for their lack of faith. These daily problems are beneficial as they produce strength for the long haul. As we remain in Jesus and repeatedly see what He accomplishes in our lives, we develop the ability to just keep on keeping on. Have a great day!

ROMANS 12:3

Do not think you are better than you are.

My little grandsons Kutler and Merrick are a hoot to fish and play with. They are really smart and pick up things really quickly. Like most kids, they are determined to do as much as they can on their own. In the boat, they are already expert fishermen, or so they think—they think they can pick out the right lure, tie it on, and make a perfect cast. This display of confidence is pretty acceptable in a child. In fact, we're glad they are so assertive and try so hard.

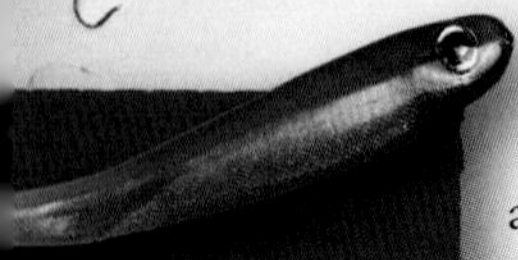

TIP

Bass located on bluffs are less affected by rising water.

For the rest of us, this attitude is generally called "pride" and is something God tells us is bad. It's easy to be humble when you fail, but difficult when you have success. When you win today, glorify God instead of yourself.

PROVERBS 15:3

The Lord's eyes see everything;
he watches both evil and good people.

Underwater cameras are all the rage now in fishing. They work incredibly well and are relatively inexpensive. I own a couple of these cameras and have seen some neat stuff when the water was fairly clear. That's the catch: you need clear water. Lights help, but clear water is the deal.

TIP
Search out pea gravel banks for spawning crappie.

How would you like to be able to really, really see everything underwater? God can. He can see everything, and He's watching both you and me right now. How would we conduct ourselves if we remembered God is sitting right beside us at work, in our car, or while we waited in line at Bass Pro or the airport? I believe we would be a little nicer, happier, friendlier, and more loving to one another. He *is* here! Let's live like it!

April 13

1 SAMUEL 6:20

Who can stand before the Lord, this holy God?

It's a lot of fun to watch people meet superstar fishermen. Most pretty much take these big-name guys in stride, but some folks get downright flustered when they meet a big fishing star. I once saw a guy get so excited meeting Bill Dance that when he introduced his son to Bill, he forgot the boy's name—his son's name, not Bill's.

I wonder what this guy might do when he stands before the biggest Name, the almighty God. How might any of us act, and what would we say and do? The truth is . . . without Jesus we're all in trouble. But praise God, He has provided the way for us to come before Him. With Jesus, we can confidently stand before the throne of God and know we will be welcomed into His family!

TIP

Throw crankbaits when the water level is falling.

April 14

JOHN 6:20

Jesus said to them, "It is I. Do not be afraid."

I ONCE HEARD a guy tell his buddy about his day with Tommy Biffle: "He put his bait in places we wouldn't even think of throwing in!" He could have been talking about any topline pro. They have the ability and confidence to attempt and make just about any cast. Learn to cast like this, and you will definitely start catching more bass.

As we go about our day-to-day affairs, we all face seemingly impossible situations from time to time. What gives me the confidence to go ahead and cast when these come along? My confidence is in Jesus and in my close personal relationship with Him. He has always seen me through the many problem times, and He's not done yet!

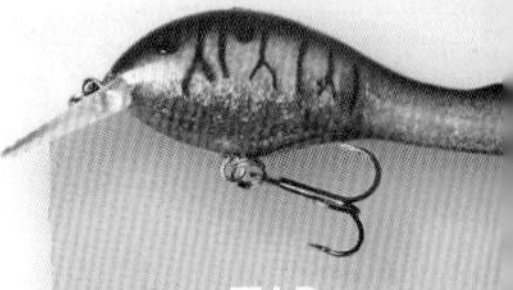

TIP

Learn to pitch and to flip to get into those really tough spots.

APRIL 15

PSALM 55:22

Give your worries to the LORD,
and he will take care of you.

A BASS ON A BED is a fish that is not going to eat anything for several days. For years, most folks thought these fish were next to impossible to catch, but we now have the lures and techniques to catch just about every bedding bass we find. The real trick is simply to worry that bass to death. Eventually the bass will bite. The more patient you become, the more success you will have.

TIP

Saltwater stripers will move into rivers to spawn.

Worries are a major problem in most folk's lives, and worry can cause many major health problems. God knew this all along and gave us His perfect answer to handling our worries: give them to Him! No matter how many or how big your worries, get in prayer right now and give them to God. He will take care of you!

April 16

MARK 3:25

"A family that is divided cannot continue."

ONE OF MY MAJOR GOALS has always been to promote family fishing. For the most part, if Dad is involving Mom and the kids in his fishing activities, that family will grow closer. So many positive things will happen while spending this time together. Obviously, we are passing on our skills. We also get into solving problems together, figuring out how to catch fish, and sharing what God has created for us to enjoy. If you are not fishing with your family, you're missing a fantastic opportunity. Nothing—not tournaments, not fishing with your buddies, nothing—is more important than the family God gave you. Take your family fishing the first chance you get.

TIP

When the dogwoods bloom, bass usually will bite a spinnerbait.

April 17

ACTS 2:4

They were all filled with the Holy Spirit.

HAVE YOU EVER NOTICED how some bass seem to put up more of a fight than others? Have you had strikes that nearly jerk the rod out of your hand while other hits are so subtle, you can hardly detect them? One of the reasons for these differences is that bass all seem to have distinct personalities. We see this all the time in our large fish tank at our store. God has even created each bass a little differently.

TIP

When the wind is from the west, the fish bite the best!

When we are saved and place our complete trust in Jesus, God places in us His Holy Spirit. This Spirit of God noticeably changes the way we act, the way we talk, the way we see others, and even the way we think. All this is for the better and for our good. God's own Spirit, living in each of us individually . . . *Wow*!

April 18

PROVERBS 14:29

Patient people have great understanding.

I'VE HEARD it said that women make better fishermen than men because they have such great patience. I don't know about that, but I do know my wife, Chris, is the best bass fisherman I have ever fished with. We've been married now for over forty-five years, so I must be a really patient man myself! (Not exactly.)

TIP

Dingy water allows you to fish closer to the fish.

All my life, I've enjoyed being impatient. I've never prayed for patience for fear that God would give it to me, but supernaturally. After all these years, God has granted me the patience I need even though I didn't request it. At the same time, He has increased my understanding. This enhances my relationship with others and, more importantly, my relationship with Him.

April 19

JOSHUA 23:15

Every good promise that the L*ORD your God has made has come true, and in the same way, his other promises will come true.*

The Ohio River around Cincinnati is not known as a great place to fish. In fact, it's pretty much known for just the opposite. A couple of my hunting buddies, Bill Epeards and Jack Gratsch, promised me a great fishing trip if I would do a television show with Jack on the Ohio. I showed up, and we fished below one of the locks and dam about twenty miles from the city. We fished Heddon Zara Spooks along the concrete walls below the locks. The hybrid bass fishing was incredible. We caught so many hybrids between five and fourteen pounds that we couldn't keep count. Sometimes it's surprising when a friend's promise comes true, but I can promise you without any doubt . . . whatever God promises will come true!

TIP

Fish the mouths of small feeder creeks that run into a river.

April 20

MARK 4:39

Jesus stood up and commanded the wind and said to the waves, "Quiet! Be still!" Then the wind stopped, and it became completely calm.

ALTHOUGH IT'S NOT NECESSARILY the best time to catch fish, all of us like the magic of a dead calm lake. Every movement and sound is magnified. We can hear and see a fish jump a couple of hundred yards away. Every movement of a topwater bait sends ripples seemingly forever. The problem is the fish can see and hear much better than we do. Rest assured, they know we're there, and that makes them harder to catch.

Think about the Jesus you believe in. He can calm the crashing waves of a raging sea. How much more can He calm the daily storms we face? This is a God so powerful He can take the fury out of any situation we face. Place your full trust in Him today.

TIP

Most really big bass live the majority of their adult lives around ten feet deep.

April 21

1 CORINTHIANS 1:25

The weakness of God is stronger than human strength.

How much fishing line should you cut off each time you retie? In the tests we did with the Berkley line tester, the line usually would break within six to eight inches of the lure. A good rule of thumb is to cut off one foot of line each time you retie. Always check your line for nicks and frays and rough spots. The weakest spot is your line strength.

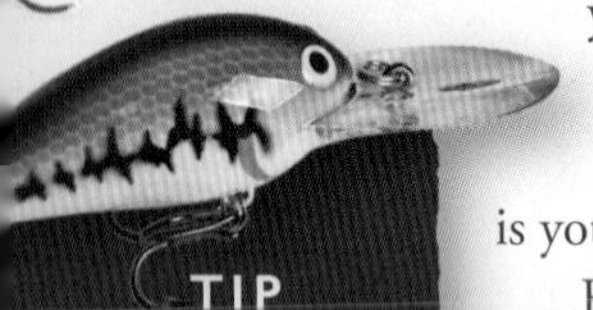

TIP

Smallmouth like open flats, five to eight feet deep, after spawning.

How strong is your biggest weakness in life, and how much does it control you? Is it money, sex, popularity, power, or something else, and is it ruining your life? If it is, identify the weakness and trade it with God for His power. It's amazing what He can do if you will only let Him. Let God's power be your ruler and your strength.

April 22

HEBREWS 10:25

You should not stay away from the church meetings, as some are doing, but you should meet together and encourage each other.

IT'S AMAZING how quickly and easily a bad day fishing can turn into a good one. It's often a tip from another angler that turns the whole day around.

TIP

Use a spinning reel to skip a worm under boat docks.

God wants us in church to benefit one another He intends for us to share our problems and our triumphs, our pain and our joy. He has promised to always be there when we meet to help this along. Will you benefit by showing up at church multiple times this week? Absolutely! Can your presence benefit others? It should. Make it a point to encourage as many folks as you can at church this week. When the week is done, you might just find you've been encouraged most of all!

April 23

HABAKKUK 2:5

Just as wine can trick a person,
those who are too proud will not last.

When you're fishing for spawning bass, it really helps to see the fish. Of course, great polarized sunglasses are a must. By seeing the bass, we know better where to place our lures. More importantly, we are able to determine the attitude of the fish. This gives us clues as how to try to catch that bass, or maybe to not even attempt a particular fish.

TIP

The only difference between a major or minor feeding period is length of time.

Pride can affect us like fishing without polarized sunglasses: it makes our vision of life cloudy, and makes us miss the mark in our actions. Pride can blur the really important things in our lives and turn us into people no one wants to be around. Rest assured, this is one of Satan's greatest tools to destroy us. Ask God today to help you battle this adversary!

April 24

PROVERBS 15:4

Healing words give life,
but dishonest words crush the spirit.

My son Jamie and I catch and haul shad to our private lake to help feed the fish. It's a difficult and delicate job because shad die so easily. We've learned many tricks, but the best is adding stock salt to the water. Before the salt, the shad look all fuzzy and sick. Add the salt, and they become sleek and healthy.

Words of hope, encouragement, and joy are like adding salt to a shad tank. They bring life and healing back to a hurting soul. We know individuals who bring those words into every conversation with everyone they meet. How great it would be if we would all strive to be one of those individuals. I'm sure going to try. How about you?

TIP

Watch the birds. They will show you where the baitfish are.

April 25

ISAIAH 62:5

As a man rejoices over his new wife,
so your God will rejoice over you.

WE ALL LIKE to talk about the good old days of fishing. We remember all the great strings of bass, crappie, and catfish we caught. Most of my best fishing memories involve my wife, Chris. After more than forty-five years of marriage, I love her now more than ever, and I thank God every day for picking her out for me.

It's impossible for us to realize how much God really loves us. Everything He has done from creation until now has been done out of His love for those He created.

It's exciting to think we can put a smile on God's face. What makes God smile? Talking to Him, reading His Word, praising and worshiping Him? Sure, but maybe most of all, it's living our lives by the example His Son, Jesus, set for us.

TIP

Sometimes teeny crankbaits will produce when all else fails.

April 26

LUKE 19:10

"The Son of Man came to find lost people and save them."

We use bait now with scents, taste, and salt. All of these help us catch fish. One downside with tubes, sinking worms, and wacky worm rigs, though, is that a lot of fish swallow the hook. I fish most of the time with barbless hooks. So even when a bass swallows the bait and hook, I can remove it without killing the bass.

God's desire is that we all be saved by His Son, Jesus. Jesus accomplished much on this earth, performed great miracles, and taught tremendous life lessons. His purpose, however, was to die on that cross to pay for your sins and mine. He rose again to life to prove we could also be saved from death and live forever with Him. He has forever removed the barbs of sin and death.

TIP

Search out points in submerged weed lines with your depth finder.

April 27

JOB 41:11

No one has ever given [God] anything that [he] must pay back.

We spend a lot of money and invest a lot of time trying to become better fishermen and catch more fish. We all get excited when we hear about a new lure or technique. We're making this investment in hopes of a greater return in fish catches.

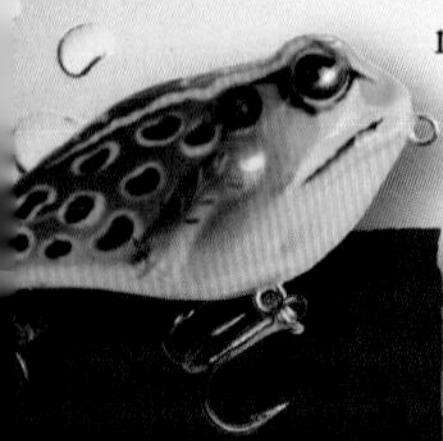

TIP

Follow up missed buzzbait strikes with a slow rolled spinnerbait or tube.

We often play the same game with God. We mentally expect to get what we want and receive His blessings in abundance. After all, we tithe, we teach, we attend, we witness, we support. Doesn't God owe us something in return? Not at all. Everything we have, including our money, time, and talents, are already gifts of love from God. What we choose to give back to Him must be gifts of our love to Him!

April 28

1 SAMUEL 10:9

When Saul turned to leave Samuel,
God changed Saul's heart.

I FIRST MET George W. Bush when his dad was vice president under Ronald Reagan. We first fished together when he was running for governor of Texas. Perhaps his most enduring quality is how genuine he is: what you see is what you get. President Bush wears his faith in God on his sleeve and has taken much criticism for this. I remember him once saying God changed his heart. Fact is, that's exactly what God does when we turn our lives over to Him.

TIP

Wake a spinnerbait on riprap early in the morning.

If you're not really the kind of person you want to be, the heart is the place to start. Most of us don't have a clue about making this change. The Master Heart Surgeon is standing by right now, just waiting on your call to Him.

April 29

HEBREWS 11:1

Faith means being sure of the things we hope for and knowing that something is real even if we do not see it.

THE EASIEST WAY to get a mental picture of an underwater creek or roadbed is with ten to twelve marker buoys. Crisscross over the creek or road and drop a buoy each time you cross. Quickly, you have the creek or road laid out with buoys on the top of the water. Now you know what it looks like and can easily see key areas to fish. This increases our faith in the particular structure.

TIP

Crawdads will reappear in the early fall as food for the fish.

I'm not sure there is a shortcut to real faith in Jesus. If there is, it's the fact that God chose us and He's working in us and for us every day. We don't see God, but we see the results of His presence. Just like we're really not seeing that creek. We're only seeing marker buoys, but we know the creek is there. I see God's work, and I know Jesus is there.

APRIL 30

ACTS 20:35

I taught you to remember the words Jesus said: "It is more blessed to give than to receive."

WIVES OF TOURNAMENT FISHERMEN must be a special class of women. What a demanding job and what a great asset to any tournament angler. Chris helps drive the rig to the tournament, practices with me, helps me locate fish, keeps my boat clean, and winds new line—all this before the tournament even starts. Many wives homeschool the kids while on the road. All this and each wife is still her husband's biggest encourager and number one fan.

TIP
The calmer the water, the slower you need to work your topwater.

Why do these ladies do all this giving? Love! Each woman loves her fisherman, and her joy is helping him and seeing him do well. God loves us enough to give His Son to save us from an eternity in hell. His giving enables us to come before Him cleansed of sin and ready to spend forever in paradise.

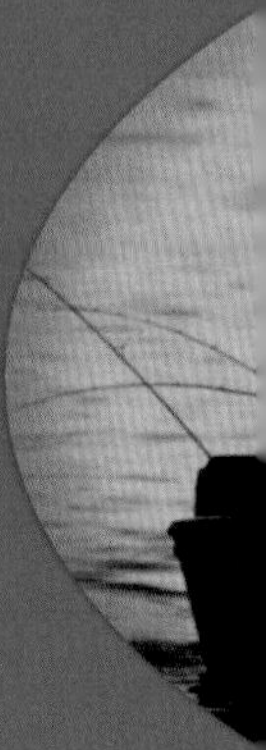

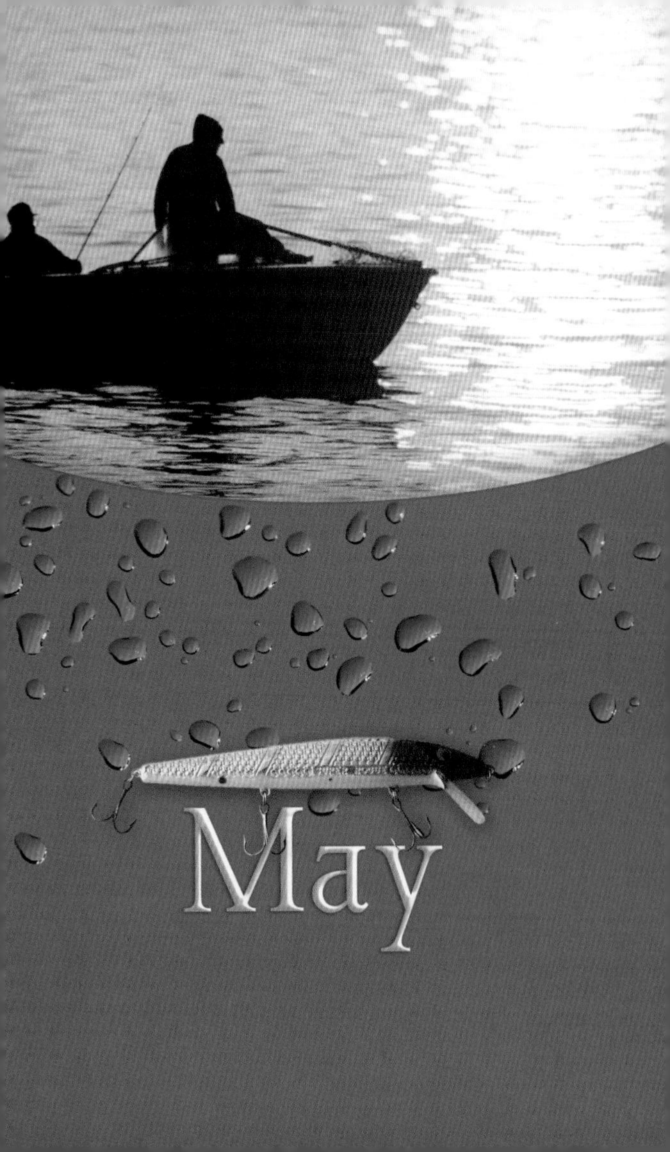
May

May 1

PSALM 32:5

I confessed my sins to you
and didn't hide my guilt. . . .
and you forgave my guilt.

In a recent BASS tournament, my close friend Mark Menendez broke one of the tournament rules. Although no one knew except Mark, he turned himself in to tournament officials and was disqualified. Mark showed great integrity, but still paid the price. He didn't cheat; he simply violated a rule by accident.

TIP
Small edges of shade along bluffs will hold fish.

We all violate God's rules. And, yes, these violations carry a penalty. God knows every time we sin. We're not telling Him anything new when we confess our sin; what we are doing is humbling ourselves before God. This is what God requires. This is where my God gets really great. He forgives my violation, erases my guilt, and does not disqualify me.

JOHN 6:27

"Work for the food that stays good always and gives eternal life."

FISHING IS JUST A GAME, but if you ever want to get really good at this game, you've really got to put in a lot of work. This comes pretty easily for most of us because of our passion for fishing. We get up early and spend hours standing and making cast after cast. It's hard work, but we love it because we love fishing.

The work God is asking of us is that we believe in His Son, Jesus Christ. The food that produces eternal life is prayer, reading God's Word, and assembling with God's people. We often try to feed our spiritual hunger with worldly food, music, entertainment, movies, and the like. This leaves our souls hungry and our hearts empty. Fill up today with the food of God's love. If Jesus can feed five thousand people on a mountaintop, He can certainly feed you and me.

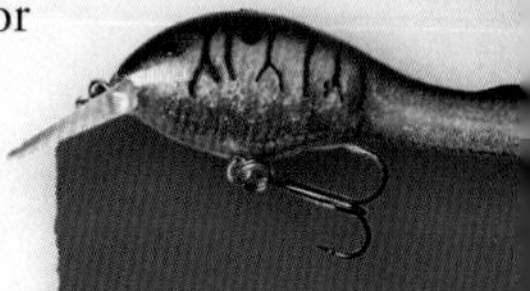

TIP

Always wear polarized sunglasses while fishing.

MAY 3

2 KINGS 20:5

I have heard your prayer and seen your tears, so I will heal you.

MAY IS ONE of the really great months to fish in most of America. You have fish in pretty much all stages of the spawn, and you can catch bass in a variety of ways. Pick your favorite lure and technique, put your foot on your Minn Kota, and get after it. At the end of the day, you should have some great string-stretching memories. If only May could last forever. . .

TIP

Jerkbaits, such as Rogues, produce well over deeper points after the spawn.

God has allotted each of us only so many Mays and just a certain number of days. Through King Hezekiah, God gives us an example of adding to one's life. It's one of my favorite Bible stories as God adds years to the king's life. What a great example of the power of prayer. Proof positive, God answers prayer and nothing is too tough for Him to handle.

JOSHUA 8:1

The LORD said to Joshua. "Don't be afraid or give up."

MUDDY WATER scares a lot of bass fishermen. When you look at water with coon tracks on top, it can be pretty frightening. The bass, on the other hand, don't mind at all. They're well equipped with great senses to survive in muddy water. They actually can see much better than you would imagine.

TIP

Occasionally check and tighten the lug nuts on your boat trailer.

When fishing in muddy water, it's important to remember three key things—shallow, shallow, shallow. The shallower you fish, the more bites you'll get.

Jesus continually told His disciples not to be afraid. He knows that fear is a natural response. We are not sure what's going to happen in a scary situation. Our comfort is that Jesus does know the outcome. He also knows that He will help us and see us through. In fact, He will even bring us through death itself.

May 5

TITUS 2:2

Teach older men to be self-controlled, serious, wise, strong in faith, in love, and in patience.

It's amazing how many youngsters are taught to fish by their granddads. It's true, granddads probably have more time, but mostly they have great teaching qualities. I know of no dad who is as patient and self-controlled with his kids as their grandfather is with them. This is designed by God. As we grow older, God is at work building us into the men He desires us to be.

TIP

The bigger the crankbait, the bigger the bass.

As you look through the qualities in the scripture above, measure each one in yourself. If you find that you're lacking any or all of the attributes, ask God specifically to help you. You'll find that He will supernaturally. After all, that's what He wants for you anyway.

2 CORINTHIANS 9:8

And God can give you more blessings than you need. Then you will always have plenty of everything—enough to give to every good work.

OVER THE YEARS, we have held many events with the FOCAS group that required a lot of volunteer help. What a blessing it was to know that there would always be just enough volunteers to do what needed to be done. For tournaments, there would be just enough prizes; for the Kid's Day, we would always manage to get just enough people to make sure everything went smoothly. Many hours went into the preparation, and there were times it just didn't look like it was going to come together. But in all those years, we never had a rain-out for either event. God definitely was in control, and He blessed the hands that were willing to work.

TIP

Take time to learn how to interpret your fish locators.

May 7

1 PETER 4:12

My friends, do not be surprised at the terrible trouble which now comes to test you.

CHRIS AND I found a little patch of fish one week on a small flat on the bed of a creek. The spot was only about fifty yards long, but was loaded with good bass. For three straight days we caught six to ten bass every time we fished this special honey hole. Then it rained four or five inches. The lake came up six feet, and we couldn't buy a bite on that spot.

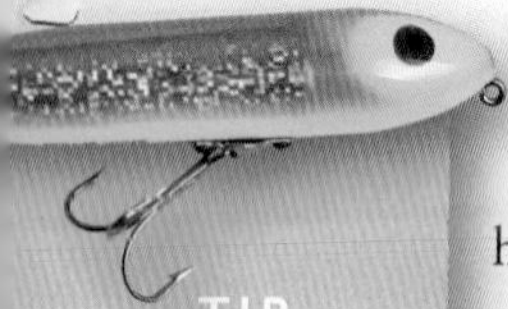

TIP

Search out small city lakes for some surprisingly good fishing.

The Bible tells us we will have terrible times that will come along. Most all of us have already been there and know they will come again. That's just how life is. So how do we make it through these tests? We make it by God's amazing grace. He has mountains and mountains of grace He is just waiting to give to His chosen ones. When terrible trouble happens, God will always be right there, on the spot, with enough amazing grace to see us through.

MATTHEW 25:45

"I tell you the truth, anything you refused to do even for the least of my people here, you refused to do for me."

IT'S A HELPLESS FEELING to break down on the water. Sometimes you're miles from where you launched, floating around with no help in sight. What a relief when you see a boat coming. What a sinking feeling when the driver doesn't see you or pretends not to see you and looks the other way. Fortunately, most folks will stop and give you a tow.

But unfortunately, we do live in a society where we increasingly look the other way. Jesus says that when we do this, we are turning our backs on Him. Jesus went out of His way to help those who needed help the most. He expects us to do the same. When you look at someone in need, you're actually looking into the face of Jesus. As people of Christ, we should be first in line to help.

TIP

Use a bobber to suspend a Road Runner over submerged brush piles.

May 9

LAMENTATIONS 3:25

The Lord is good to those who hope in him,
to those who seek him.

Finding fish after they spawn can be pretty difficult. The fish don't necessarily stay shallow, but they won't automatically go deep. Most suspend four or five feet deep, but this can be in a wide variety of places depending on the type of water you are fishing. They might be in over thirty feet of water on points or in the tops of willow trees at five or six feet deep. You get the picture?

Finding God is much easier to do no matter where you are or who you are. God is right there with you right now. All you need to do is to seek Him. Get in prayer and talk to God; get personal and intimate with Him. Pretty quickly you'll start to see just how good the God you hope in really is.

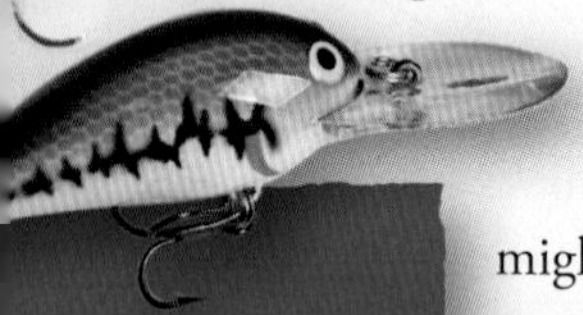

TIP

Illinois pondweed (duckweed) has thick stems that provide great underwater cover.

May 10

JUDGES 10:15

We have sinned. Do to us whatever you want, but please save us today.

Lake Hamilton in Hot Springs, Arkansas, is one of the city lakes that has super fishing. One of the overlooked fisheries here is catfish. Because Hamilton is a high usage lake with lots of houses, restaurants, and marinas, it has tons of lights. These lights are a great attractant for bugs and baitfish. Make a bet, the catfish will show up pretty much every night.

TIP

Catfish will feed under gar rolling on top during spawning season.

Our sins are out in the light 24/7 to God. Nothing we do is hidden from Him. Knowing this, why should we even try to hide our sins from God? Our sins create consequences and produce bad results. These bad situations will continue until we put ourselves under God's control and will. Yes, we will be punished for our sins, and then only God can and will save us.

EXODUS 23:2

You must not do wrong just because everyone else is doing it.

HAVE YOU NOTICED that when a hot new lure comes out, it's not long until every other company has one just like it! Sometimes the imitations sell better and catch more fish than the original. This is, indeed, a copycat business.

TIP

Black perch make great trotline bait for large early season catfish.

Unfortunately this need to imitate is a by-product of human nature. We tend to follow the group, whether it's right or wrong, moral or immoral. One of the biggest falsehoods in our morality and values is that if everyone is doing it, it must be okay.

The truth is, wrong is wrong, and right is not to be compromised just because everyone else does. Our values, our morals, our rules for life come from God.

As God's people we simply must live by God's law and not be swayed by the thinking and actions of everyone else.

May 12

MARK 10:45

"The Son of Man did not come to be served. He came to serve others."

We do a lot of entertaining on our ranch in southern Oklahoma. Some of it is for business, but most is just sharing with our friends. Chris cooks and serves great meals, and we work extra hard to make these visits special. We have to help some people get in the boat because of age or physical limitations. We tie on hooks, rig baits, land and unhook fish, pick out backlashes, and so forth. Sometimes we even throw the lure out for the beginning anglers. We do this because we love these friends. All of them have shown a special love for us, and seeing them happy is our reward.

TIP

Screw down a magnet on your front deck to hold your needle nose and cutters.

Jesus has a special love for each of us. His desire is to serve our every need, not for just a day or week, not for a lifetime, but for eternity.

May 13

PHILIPPIANS 2:1

Does your life in Christ give you strength?

THE MORE YOU FISH, the stronger certain muscles become. Your legs, your arms, your wrists . . . well, that's the theory, but the older you get, the more you prove this premise wrong. I'm fishing more now than at any time since college, yet it seems I hurt more now than ever. But I know that without the work of fishing, I'd be in nowhere near as good a shape.

TIP

In extremely heavy cover, mash your barbs down on a Road Runner.

God wants us to keep ourselves strong. He really intends for our lives to be filled with strength and power—the strength to overcome all of life's ups and downs, the strength to succeed when failure seems inevitable. This is what life in Christ is all about. My God delivers when everything else I've relied on has failed. God doesn't dump this strength on us in one big pile. He gives it out just as we need it.

2 TIMOTHY 1:7

God did not give us a spirit that makes us afraid but a spirit of power and love and self-control.

One of the tricks to fishing heavy cover is short casts. This knowing how to pitch and flip comes in handy. When the fish are so secure in heavy cover, we can get in really close and not spook them.

God places His Holy Spirit in us to keep us from fear. He gives us this Spirit of confidence and power—God's power. His Spirit also produces benefits—love and self-control. How do we get this amazing Spirit? Can we order it off television? How much do we pay? Are there shipping and handling charges? Actually, God gives this Spirit of power, love, and self-control to everyone He saves. This is the "Wait! There's more" part of salvation. Ask God to let His Spirit work in you today.

TIP

Practice flipping and pitching with a coffee cup.

May 15

PROVERBS 15:4

Dishonest words crush the spirit.

WE'VE GOT HUNDREDS of bluegill and perch that hang out at our dock. My grandkids love to catch these fish. They like to use Berkley Crappie Nibbles. This is a prepared PowerBait that we use to tip Road Runners. With a small hook, it's dynamite for these small panfish. The problem is that the little ones steal the bait often without the kids even knowing they had a bite.

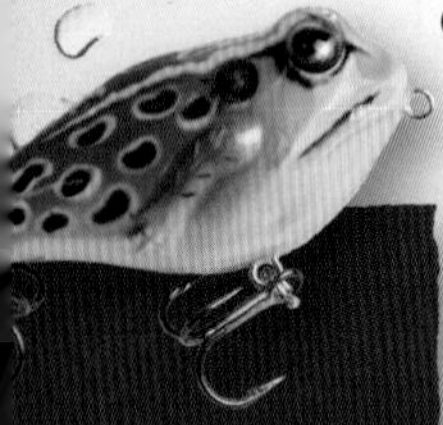

TIP

Rattles often produce extra bites on a plastic worm.

There's a little built-in larceny in everyone. The devil uses this to hurt others, especially in what we say. Words can be more damaging than physical pain. If the truth hurts, how much more a lie? Be extra careful to not let Satan lead you into a falsehood. After all, God wants us to build up, not crush.

MAY 16

JONAH 4:6

The LORD made a plant grow quickly up over Jonah, which gave him shade.

RECENTLY I HAD the pleasure of fishing with two young men from "Hunt of a Lifetime," Trevor Smith and his brother, Cody. Both of these guys are really good fishermen and very competitive. Because of a recent bone marrow transplant, Trevor could only stay out in the sun for short periods of time. The forecast for our outing was 90 degrees and sunny, but the first morning it rained so hard, we couldn't even fish until noon! The sun did peek out a time or two, but not for long. The second morning, it was crystal clear at 6:30 a.m. By 7:30, a few clouds rolled in, and by 8:00, solid clouds and a light rain. We caught more than a hundred bass those two days.

TIP

Go early, stay late.

Does my God care enough about one twelve-year-old boy to send those needed clouds? You bet your last rod and reel He does!

May 17

1 THESSALONIANS 4:16

The Lord himself will come down from heaven with a loud command.

BOB FERRIS was the booming voice of Bass'n Gals for twenty-one years. He had one of those voices that was almost a melody when he spoke; he was almost singing. In addition, his voice really carried.

TIP

As you move into warmer weather, use smaller worms.

When Jesus returns, it literally will be the shout heard around the world. Every man, woman, and child—inside or outside—will hear the voice of the almighty God. Indeed, all mankind will tremble. Many will try to run and hide. Some really won't understand what is happening. For those of us who have received redemption from that same Jesus, it will be the moment of ultimate victory. And, yes, I sure would like to still be alive here on this earth to experience that moment.

MATTHEW 15:28

Jesus answered, "Woman, you have great faith! I will do what you asked."

As a kid, I pretty much tried to beg into every fishing and hunting trip my dad went on. He took me fishing most of the time, but hunting trips took more asking. Dad started taking me way before I was big enough to carry a gun, and as I grew older, Dad's answer was almost always yes.

As we grow as believers in Christ, we also grow in faith that God will answer our requests with a yes. When this happens, you'll notice yourself including God in the smaller matters in your life, not just major problems. That's just what God wants. In fact, He demands it. Realize that God, in order to be your God, must be involved daily in all the facets of your life. Only then can God's will really be done.

TIP

Spray Reel Magic on all your electrical connections in your boat about once a month.

May 19

HEBREWS 4:15

When [Jesus lived on earth], he was tempted in every way that we are, but he did not sin.

A WARM, beautiful spring day to a fisherman is like a picnic basket to Yogi Bear. Old Yogi would do just about anything to get that basket. And fishermen will do pretty much anything to go fishing on one of those special spring days! And, yes, I've skipped class, work, responsibilities, and even church to go fishing. Surely almost all of us can identify here.

TIP

After a rain you can stock up on nightcrawlers in most city parks without having to dig.

Jesus walked on earth more than thirty years as man. He faced the same daily temptations of any man, yet He remained God and faced these temptations without sinning. His power? His Father's Word! Whatever temptation confronts you today—and you will be confronted by something—God's Word can also be your power. The more immersed we are in the Word, the more capable we become of handling temptations.

MAY 20

NUMBERS 11:29

I wish the LORD would give his Spirit to all of them!

IT'S WILD sometimes to watch some sort of live bait fall into the water . . . a crawdad, frog, grasshopper, spider, and the like. We expect a fish to instantly explode on the real thing. Sometimes it happens, but often the bait safely reaches shore. It succeeds by trying to not look like or act like a crawdad, frog, grasshopper, or spider. Ironically, we're trying to make our artificial bait look and act like the real live bait.

TIP

Add a rattle to your spinnerbait in muddy water.

Satan, along with all his followers, was thrown from heaven for trying to be God. Isn't it amazing that God had already planned to give His Holy Spirit to those who would believe in His Son, Jesus? Awesome!

May 21

EXODUS 16:11

Then you will know I am the LORD your God.

ONE OF THE THINGS that bugs me the most is letting a fish swallow the hook on a plastic worm or tube. Barbless hooks make it easier to get the hook out without harming the bass. I hate killing bass! The problem is knowing when there's a fish on the line. This is especially difficult in grass such as coontail. Some strikes are so subtle, and some bass, especially the big ones, suck in the hook so quickly, they're easy to miss.

TIP

When in doubt . . . set the hook!

In some ways we miss the grace of God; our Lord has been missed and not recognized by a lot of mankind throughout the years. Even as He walked on earth, most people did not know He was the Christ. Just as today, many know about Him, but deny Him. God desires that all know Him as Lord as He is still at work today drawing us to Himself.

May 22

MATTHEW 22:37

"Love the Lord your God with all your heart, all your soul, and all your mind."

CHRIS GOT TICKLED at our granddaughter, Jordyn, a while back. You see, at that time, she was almost seven and had already caught lots of fish. As she was catching bluegill after bluegill one day, she looked up at Chris and said, "Grandma Chris, I just love fishing here at Twin Eagle [Ranch]." She was having a terrific time.

There are many facets to what we call *love*. What does God want? I believe God desires the most complete love we can imagine—love that rises above material things, hobbies, careers, even family. Do we really love God that much? How can we? By understanding that all else we love is a gift from God. Without God's love for us and His mighty blessings, we have nothing, including our next breath.

TIP

A fish feeder will enhance your fishing in any body of water.

May 23

GALATIANS 6:2

By helping each other with your troubles,
you truly obey the law of Christ.

FISHERMEN ARE BOTH the best and the worst when it comes to helping. The same guy who will stop and tow a total stranger with motor problems will lie to his best friend about where and how he is catching fish and what on! What's wrong with that picture?

TIP

When cleaning a lot of crappie or white bass, set the trigger to "constant" on your filet knife.

Well, it's all about agendas. We know we need to reach out and help, but we're only willing to serve if it doesn't affect our agendas or successes. Our friend is a threat to our own fishing success. The stranger is not.

The agenda of Jesus was not only to help, but to *solve* the troubles of others. Jesus put the problems of others above His own. Helping one another is a form of obedience to God, and He really knows how to bless us when we are obedient to Him.

May 24

HEBREWS 12:14

*Try to live in peace with all people,
and try to live free from sin.*

We play in a sport where there's not much confrontation among competitors. Unlike most sports where intense rivalry, verbal abuse, and even fights happen regularly, tournament fishing is pretty tame. However, some of the younger fishermen get out of line occasionally, and a few get bent out of shape if they believe someone is saying something negative about them. This is simply ego, but it's a tool the devil uses to destroy peace and harmony.

Pride is an especially easy and effective sin that can snowball into more and more sins. One of the best things any of us can do is humble ourselves and go make peace with someone we have a problem with. I think God will bless those people in a mighty way.

TIP

There are more fish in any given spot than you think.

MAY 25

REVELATION 22:15

Outside the city are the evil people, those who do evil magic, who sin sexually, who murder, who worship idols and who love lies and tell lies.

WHAT ARE YOU GOING TO DO when you retire?

To a lot of us, including me, retirement means we're going fishing. I've got many retired friends who fish almost every day. Almost everyone I know who is about my age is retired. The rest of us are dreaming of all those great spring days ahead when we'll fish away our retirement.

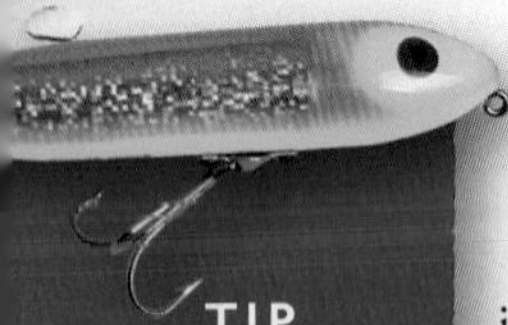

TIP

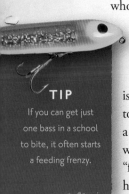

If you can get just one bass in a school to bite, it often starts a feeding frenzy.

The ultimate retirement, though, is not something that will last fifteen to twenty years, or even a hundred or a thousand years—it's forever! And we have only two places to spend that "forever"—heaven or hell. My God has made it pretty plain about who will spend their forever retirement with Him and who will spend it elsewhere. He's left the choice up to us. I know He's guaranteed my retirement in heaven with Him. How about you?

MAY 26

JEREMIAH 18:11

Stop doing evil. Change your ways and do what is right.

MOST FISHERMEN think they're pretty good at catching fish. Most believe if they really had the chance, they could make it big on the pro level. Most could not. But what they believe in their own minds is what is important.

Over the years we've blurred the lines in our minds between good and evil to the point where there is not much difference, but God draws a very well-defined line between good and evil. To God, it's adultery—not "Well, everyone does it." To God, it's murder—not a woman's choice. To God, it's a lie—not just bending the truth a bit. To God, it's divorce—not incompatibility. To God, it's stealing—not "I can't afford to tithe." It's time we wake up as a people and start doing right according to God.

TIP

Watch for the mayfly hatch, and fish near bushes and docks with mayflies.

MAY 27

PSALM 104:9

You set borders for the seas that they cannot cross.

TIDAL WATERS have always presented a challenge for me in bass fishing. Just about the time I think I've figured it out, the tide beats me again. The one thing that seems pretty constant is that low tides are better, while high tides are difficult.

Isn't it amazing how the tides work, how timely they are, and how predictable? What a mighty God who can control these huge bodies of water and move them up and down, in and out, on a daily basis! God never says "oops" and accidentally allows the tide to rise another twenty feet. He is precise with these gigantic bodies of water. We've got faith enough to build homes and business right on the waterfronts. Recognizing this power is the beginning of understanding of just how powerful God really is.

TIP

Take pictures of water at low levels to know where to fish when it rises.

May 28

ISAIAH 25:4

You protect the poor;
you protect the helpless when they are in danger.

PEACOCK BASS FISHING is probably the most exciting freshwater fishing you can do. I've fished giant Guri Lake in Venezuela many times for peacocks. It rains some almost every day, but violent storms are rare and usually end well before dark.

One time, Chris, Sherri, and I were caught twenty-five miles up the lake right at dark in an extremely violent storm. We traveled those miles in two tiny boats with no lights, no bilge pumps, and in total darkness. The storm was hot. The waves were the biggest I have ever seen, and we were never close to shore. It took more than four hours of impossible boating, but somehow our family made it. At the time, I thought our odds of safety were almost zero, but my God gave us His protection and made those odds 100 percent.

TIP
Fish a silver spoon fast through schooling bass.

May 29

MARK 13:13

"Those people who keep their faith until the end will be saved."

Once I made an appearance for Ranger Boats in Virginia. I was to arrive in Roanoke, take the shuttle to the hotel, and be ready to work the next morning. My day had started at 5 a.m., and I was looking forward to a good night's sleep ahead. My last plane was late, so I arrived at 12:30 a.m. The hotel shuttle had closed. No taxi in sight. Called a taxi and waited for thirty minutes. No problem. In my room by 1:45 a.m.—a smoking room. I've never smoked a cigarette in my life and couldn't breathe. Back to the front desk. No nonsmoking rooms available. As I unpacked, no razor and no shaving cream. Ugh. In bed by 2:30 a.m. I slept with the outside door wide open and the air conditioner on high. Throughout it all, I continually asked God to keep me Christlike—and He did.

TIP

Match your crankbait color to the color of the dominant baitfish.

May 30

LUKE 11:4

"Forgive us for our sins, because we forgive everyone who has done wrong to us."

A TWO- or three-pound bass can break fishing lines several times its weight. What generally keeps this from happening is a small amount of line stretch (forgiveness) built into monofilament and the small forgiveness in our rod tips. As long as you can keep the fish from getting a straight pull on you, you'll usually land the fish.

A small amount of forgiveness can solve big, big problems in most relationships. Just as important, a little forgiveness can keep tiny problems and mess-ups from festering into major issues. The devil hates it when you forgive. You can ruin his day anytime with forgiveness. When you do, God steps in and rewards you with His blessings. In fact, you will feel better and receive more blessing than the person you forgave.

TIP

Try swimming a tube through suspended baitfish.

MAY 31

1 CORINTHIANS 6:13

The body is not for sexual sin but for the Lord.

THE ORIGINAL Heddon Zara Spook is a bait you need to sort of work yourself into. By this I mean to fish it for a few minutes at a time, extending the time as you go. It will take awhile, but you'll soon be able to "walk the dog" with a Spook all day if necessary. We actually strengthen the exact muscles needed to fish this bait.

TIP

Spotted bass like rock piles and humps.

God perfectly created our bodies to be able to do certain things. He also warns about all types of sins that will destroy the bodies He created. Premarital sex and adultery can lead to sexually transmitted diseases, such as AIDS, that have devastating effects on our bodies. God created our bodies to do wonderful things for us and for Him. Let's keep them that way.

June

June 1

1 TIMOTHY 5:25

Good deeds are easy to see, but even those that are not easily seen cannot stay hidden.

MOST OF US really like to brag when we've done something good. Probably no national bass tournament ever has been won without some local angler telling anyone who would listen that he told the winner where to fish or told him about the winning lure.

TIP

Locate points on submerged weed lines. These can be real sweet spots.

When we do good, we really don't need to be concerned about being noticed or getting a pat on the back. God sees, God knows, and God has promised to reward every good deed. I think He probably has a greater reward for those good deeds we keep secret than those everyone knows about. Try to do something especially good today and keep it just between you and God. Then wait and see what happens.

June 2

TITUS 3:6

God poured out richly upon us that Holy Spirit through Jesus Christ our Savior.

FEW FISHERMEN can deny there is a God. Look around at any body of water on an early summer day. The steam rises, baitfish dimple the surface, and an occasional explosion signifies a big bass having breakfast. A deer with a spotted fawn walks along the shore. The best fisherman of all, a blue heron or kingfisher catches yet another bluegill. Glance up and watch as a redtail hawk circles. Look higher and an American bald eagle soars. Can you feel it? Can you feel God's Spirit in you? Oh, what rushes this God of ours shares!

TIP

Use a black Bucktail Skirt on your spinnerbait at night.

PROVERBS 12:10

Good people take care of their animals.

I HAVE A REAL PASSION for the fish in our private lake and for the deer and turkey on our land. When the lake floods, Chris and I go to the "hole" below the dam and catch the bass that have gone through the spillway tube. If we don't, they'll die of starvation. We catch these bass and put them back in the lake.

If you have a body of water you fish—a pond or a creek—take care of it. God expects you to take care of the creation over which He gave you dominion. Even if you don't own the water but merely have permission to fish, put out a feeder, feed the fish, fertilize the water. If we take care of the little places we fish, we will have lots more and bigger fish to catch.

TIP

Shad concentrate in certain sections of a creek. Find the shad, find the fish.

JOB 38:36

Who put wisdom inside the mind or understanding in the heart?

HOW MUCH OF FISHING is luck and how much is skill? Just like any other activity or sport, luck does play a part in any given day's success, but luck alone will not make you a good fisherman. You need skill, knowledge, and an understanding of the fish, water, weather, and a few other factors. God has given us the ability to gain these assets. We have more available to us now than ever to help us improve, but perhaps nothing helps us more than getting out on the water and putting our information to work.

TIP

When wading, shuffle your feet to avoid drop-offs.

On your next fishing trip, take along someone you've never fished with and pay close attention. You both will learn.

June 5

1 KINGS 3:25

[Solomon] said, "Cut the living baby into two pieces and give each woman half."

ANYONE WITH BASIC KNOWLEDGE of the Bible probably knows the end of this story. The mother of the living baby would rather give up the baby than see him die. The mother of the dead baby would just as soon see the living baby die. He's not hers—and if she can't get what she wants, then no one else should either.

TIP
A Hamby's keel protector will enhance the resale value of your boat.

What are we willing to give up in order to get what we want? Like the mother of the dead baby, many people are willing to compromise their beliefs if it means they get their way. Our values really mean nothing if we are willing to compromise them. Most of us have opportunities every day to show those around us what we stand for and what we believe. All too often I'm guilty of not standing on the firm ground God has given me. How about you?

MALACHI 3:10

"Bring to the storehouse a full tenth of what you earn so there will be food in my house. Test me in this," says the Lord All-Powerful. "I will open the windows of heaven for you and pour out all the blessings you need."

FISHERMEN HAVE REACHED the point where the price of fishing lures doesn't seem to matter. As long as we believe we have a good chance to catch a fish, we'll gladly fork out the big bucks for a hot new lure. Even minnows and red worms now can cost $2 or $3 per dozen. It's good that we have titanium split rings (LureSavers) that release the hook and allow us to get our high-dollar plugs back.

TIP

There is generally a tremendous amount of food and forage on ripraps.

We gladly pay hard-earned dollars for fish bait, but only a small percent of Christians tithe. We could list lots of reasons, but the fact remains that when we fail to tithe, we are showing dishonor to the very God who gave us the money in the first place. Truth is, when we honor God, He will honor us even more.

June 7

LUKE 4:13

After the devil had tempted Jesus in every way, he left him to wait until a better time.

The solunar tables are based on a lunar day (24 hours, 50 minutes) and help give us the major and minor feeding periods for fish and wildlife. We want to be in our best spots during these feeding periods. Fishing in the right spot at the right time is what we're all looking for each time we go out.

TIP

In fairly open water, turn your trailer hooks upside down on spinnerbaits and buzzbaits.

Similarly, the devil is always looking for the right time to cause us problems. Satan's desire is for terrible things to happen in our lives. He also knows exactly when to attack and tempt us. Maybe when we're short on money or having family problems or health problems. Satan will try to catch us at our weakest moments and lead us into sin. Your Jesus and mine has been there. Use His strength to guide you through these temptations. Satan will soon be gone!

JUNE 8

REVELATION 20:15

Anyone whose name was not found written in the book of life was thrown into the lake of fire.

GROWING UP on the Cleveland County, Oklahoma, line gave me opportunities to fish almost every day. Lightning Creek ran right behind the house, and I had three decent-size ponds within bicycle range.

TIP

When you catch a bass, re-fish the spot with another lure.

When the preacher began to talk about hell being a lake of fire, I visualized those ponds and Lightning Creek on fire. If Jesus could keep me out of hell and the lake of fire, I needed Jesus.

Today, we see these big pipeline and refinery explosions. These also might be a close picture of hell. Personally, I'll never know. I've been saved from hell by Jesus. He died for you and me and paid for the sins that would throw us into hell. My name is in that Book of Life! Is yours?

June 9

PHILEMON 1:6

I pray that the faith you share may make you understand every blessing we have in Christ.

WATCHING FOLKS on television catch fish can often cloud what most fishing trips really are. In a single, thirty-minute program, we see fish after fish being caught, and sometimes they're all whoppers. Well, we're actually seeing an all-day trip condensed into sort of a highlight show. Plus, nobody on television shows us the bad days . . . only the great days.

TIP

When trolling, use a lure that runs the same depth at which the baitfish are located.

Every day that God has given us is a great one. Every day is filled with more of God's blessings than we can count. Yet, we still find ways to dwell on whatever is wrong or might go wrong each day. God is pouring out blessings with every breath we take, yet our hearts overflow with evil. You make the choice: "Poor, pitiful me," or "Wow! What an awesome God!"

June 10

JOHN 4:14

"The water I give will become a spring of water gushing up inside that person, giving eternal life."

DETERMINING what the water is doing at any given time is one of the keys to fishing success. Is it rising, subsiding, warming, chilling, clearing up, getting muddy? Water is always doing something. Pay close attention to what the water is doing. The more you understand the water, the more fish you will catch.

TIP

Determine your hook size by the diameter of the worm, not the length.

The Bible calls Jesus "living water." Water that gives eternal life. Water that quenches your thirst forever. This means that Jesus is all we need to have life eternal with God. We don't need good looks, power, fame, or even money. All we need is faith in Jesus. Is your pitcher of faith filled with the living water of Jesus?

JUNE 11

ROMANS 7:15

I do not do what I want to do,
and I do the things I hate.

TO ME, Carolina rig worm fishing is about as close as you can get to not going fishing at all. It's a tremendous technique and really catches fish. In addition, it's really simple to learn and easy to do. But for me, it's a little like watching lilypad flowers open.

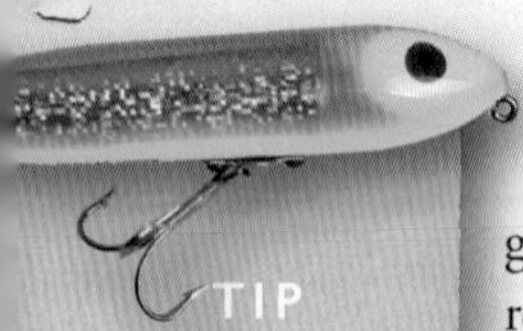

TIP

Slow a worm with a 1/8 oz. or 1/16 oz. weight over grass beds.

Paul complained in Romans that he committed sins that he hated. We're probably the most guilty of this in close, personal relationships such as with our family. We seem to treat those we love the most with the most disrespect, the most anger, and the least compassion and affection. When something goes wrong today, bite your tongue, swallow your pride, and speak words of love and encouragement instead of harsh or ugly words.

June 12

2 PETER 1:3

Jesus has the power of God, by which he has given us everything we need to live and to serve God.

HOW MANY FISHING LURES does a person need? I've never heard a definite answer, but I'm pretty sure almost all of us already have enough. Yet, we still want more. We still buy more.

I guess fishing lures are like just about everything else we have. God has supplied our needs, yet we want more—more money, more success, more kids, more grandkids, more land, more this, more that. We can all build wish lists a mile long. Instead, how about building a "Thanks, God" list of what we do have? Mine would start with my salvation, my family, my health, and then I could go for pages without ever reaching the end of the list. God gives everything we wish for and more!

TIP

When bass begin schooling on shad, use a multi-blade spinnerbait.

JUNE 13

LUKE 6:38

"Give and you will receive. . . . The way you give to others is the way God will give to you."

FISHING PROVIDES wonderful opportunities to share with others. We can share our time, our skills, and our experiences. I believe wholeheartedly the more we give to anything, the more we receive back. This is God's plan. This principle goes way beyond tangible things. It includes attitudes and feelings. The morc love we give, the more we'll be loved.

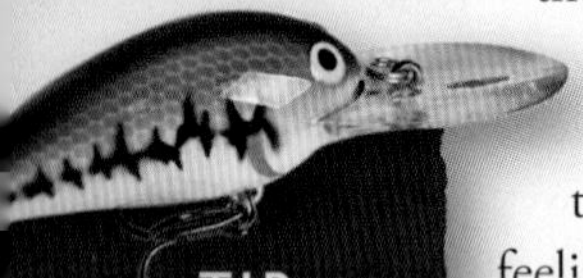

TIP

For suspended deep water bass, try a float-n-fly technique.

Do you want to be happy? Then give happiness to others. It's amazing how even a simple smile will cause folks to smile back. The results are gifts from God. This deal of God's works both ways. If we give bitterness, anger, harsh words, lies, or anything else bad or negative, that's usually what we'll receive back.

June 14

1 TIMOTHY 1:16

Christ Jesus could show that he has patience without limit.

A FLOAT TRIP down one of America's rivers or streams is a wonderful experience in late spring or early summer. God has filled the woods to their fullest with green, and the power of His presence seems to be in that moving water.

The next time you have an opportunity to experience this kind of fishing, consider your salvation. Think about the day God saved you and became King of your life. If you have any doubts about whether or not you're actually saved, that's okay. Maybe God has been patiently waiting for this moment for you to come to Him. God's saving power is certain, and He wants to make sure you know you've received it!

TIP

Live frogs are excellent for all species of freshwater fish—especially big catfish.

June 15

COLOSSIANS 1:13

God has freed us from the power of darkness, and he brought us into the kingdom of his dear Son.

Bass feed at night. In fact, many really big bass become all but impossible to catch during daylight hours.

Although darkness is our friend when it comes to fishing, God equates darkness with Satan and his fallen-angel demons. God has even allowed Satan to have awesome worldly power on earth. The devil's power may be greater now in the United States of America than at any other time.

If you're saved as a Christian who claims Jesus as your Lord, you're set apart and no longer held captive to the devil's power. Satan will still cause problems, but Jesus will never let these destroy you. Instead, God will use these difficulties to strengthen you.

TIP

Really big poppers catch few fish other than really big bass. Try the Cordell Pencil Popper.

June 16

PROVERBS 11:2

Pride leads only to shame;
it is wise to be humble.

TOURNAMENT BASS FISHING will humble any fisherman. The very nature of the game invites failure. Talk about baseball being a poor percentage game—get three hits for every ten times at bat and make the Hall of Fame. How many casts does it take to catch three bass? I'd take three out of a hundred every day.

TIP
Try a scum frog beneath trees and around hard cover during the summertime.

We often equate humility with weakness and failure, but God says humility is a good thing that produces wisdom. How can that be? I believe humility changes our perspective. It forces us to look at and rely more on God and less on ourselves. So many times, I simply reach the end of the day and have run out of solutions, but God has always been faithful to see me through.

June 17

PROVERBS 28:22

Selfish people are in a hurry to get rich
and do not realize they soon will be poor.

SOMETIMES A BASS will grab your bait and swim off at warp speed. That's a great indication of more bass in that spot. You might have just found a real honey hole. Bass are selfish. They have no desire to share their food. A momma bass won't even share with her own babies.

TIP

Windy days will blow grasshoppers into the water. A Rebel CrickHopper will imitate the real thing.

God warns often about our selfish desires to store up worldly riches. I, personally, try to mask that desire by calling it *security*: I'm storing up for the bad times that may come. But God wants you and me to share what we have with others and with Him. Sharing is Christlike; selfishness is devilkin. The frightening part is when we realize that selfishness will drive us to poverty.

June 18

REVELATION 21:4

He will wipe away every tear from their eyes, and there will be no more death, sadness, crying, or pain.

FISH FEEL NO PAIN. Contrary to what the anti-fishing folks proclaim, those hooks don't hurt the fish at all. We, on the other hand, feel pain in so many ways—physically, spiritually, emotionally. We have lots of ways to hurt, and it will always be that way here on Earth.

TIP

Use a fishing log to remember details and make you a better fisherman.

Here at our tiny company, our team experienced four deaths in four days running. At such times of sorrow, we are forced to keep our eyes and hearts and minds focused on Jesus. Remember that God has promised a city of no pain, no crying, no sickness of any kind, and no death. God calls it heaven. It's reserved for you, for me, and for everyone who calls upon Jesus to be saved. It's also more incredible than we can imagine—but, oh, what joy to try!

June 19

1 CORINTHIANS 10:13

You can trust God, who will not permit you to be tempted more than you can stand. . . . He will also give you a way to escape.

Another Jimmy Houston rule of thumb: find the heaviest cover near deep water. The heavy cover gives a bass a great ambush point toward forage, not a place to hide. The deep water provides an escape when they're startled or in danger.

TIP

Take time to invite an old friend fishing.

Trusting Jesus will not make you immune from temptation. In fact, it makes you a target, and Satan may work on you even harder with even greater temptations. But when you feed on God's Word and then seek safety in the depths of your faith in God, He will defend you. Prayer is another great weapon we have to fight through temptation. All too often, my problem is enjoying these little temptations. The danger is they're just like a small seed of sin that has a great ability to grow. Don't give them the chance.

June 20

JOB 42:10

After Job had prayed for his friends, the LORD gave him success again.

IN THE 1970S, we fished a BASS national tournament on Cherokee Lake in Tennessee. Cherokee was an incredibly difficult lake. There wasn't much cover, the water was clear, and the bass population was pretty thin. I fished against a local man named Cecil. He did pretty well in the tournament, and his first day's partner caught the big bass of the tournament on Cecil's water.

TIP

Never give up. Many tournaments are won in the last hour.

Cecil and I didn't meet in that tournament, but he remembered me and followed us on television for years. I recently visited Cecil in Jonesville, Tennessee. He had been diagnosed with emphysema and was bedridden. As I knelt by his bed, held his hand, and prayed with him, I was overcome by how much God loves and cares for each one of His children.

June 21

HOSEA 6:1

Come, let's go back to the Lord.

DURING A PRACTICE DAY for a BASS tournament in New Orleans, Chris and I fished several hundred yards of cypress trees. It should have been a dynamite spot, but I only caught one three-pound bass on a Cordell Hot Spot. I didn't return to the area until the last twenty minutes of the tournament. I had a limit, but I needed one decent kicker fish. I didn't catch that exact fish, but I did catch one that was close to three pounds, and that helped almost as much.

TIP

Try moving to larger hooks with LureSaver split rings on your crankbaits.

You don't always find the bass you go back for, but Jesus is always waiting when you return to Him. No matter how far you've drifted, Jesus is still right there. Call on Him now. He's waiting.

June 22

MATTHEW 22:39

"Love your neighbor as you love yourself."

IF YOU HAVE the opportunity to fish a good smallmouth lake, never underestimate a spinnerbait—even in the summer. Those brown fish really love brightly colored blades. Solid chartreuse, solid white, or any combination of the same work best. You can tip any of those blades with fluorescent red, and it will really help.

Love also shines brightly and attracts others. Jesus commands us to love others as we love ourselves. What He's really telling us is to take care of the needs of others just as we would take care of our own needs. This is *showing* love, not merely *talking* love. Reach out to fill the needs of a neighbor today. Remember, your neighbor just might need Jesus, and you could be the perfect person to fill that need.

TIP

A crankbait or jerkbait can be used in a Carolina rig instead of soft plastic.

June 23

1 THESSALONIANS 4:17

And we will be with the Lord forever.

Close your eyes. Think of the best fishing water you've ever fished. Now, think about the very best day fishing you've ever had. Put those two together and remember what made that place and that day so special. Multiply that experience in your mind a few thousand times, and you might be just beginning to see what heaven is like and what being with the Lord is all about.

TIP
Look for flats that have scattered stumps near deep water.

Remember that being with the Lord forever begins the day we're saved, not the day we die. Walking with Jesus every day is a journey you don't want to miss. I wouldn't miss that fishing trip for anything in the world.

June 24

1 PETER 2:1

So then, rid yourselves of all evil, all lying, hypocrisy, jealousy, and evil speech.

A PERFECT DAY'S FISHING is hard to come by, but that's what we're looking for, isn't it? That day when both the weather and the fish really cooperate. Not much wind, not too hot, not too cold, and a biting fish in just about every good-looking spot.

Living a perfect life is even more difficult. Perfection, however, is what God wants from us and for us. How do we do that? By asking Jesus to save us, to transform us from what we are into what God wants us to be. Will we instantly become perfect? No, but our past becomes perfect, and our future will be aided by God's Holy Spirit.

We'll strive to be perfect with His help, and then one day, with the help of Jesus, we'll get there.

TIP

Bridge pilings will hold bass and crappie almost all summer long.

June 25

TITUS 3:1–2

Be ready to do good, to speak no evil about anyone, to live in peace, and to be gentle and polite to all people.

SUMMERTIME FISH are school fish. If you can locate one or two, you've probably located a bunch. One of my biggest problems is slowing down enough to really work on the school. I've a bad habit of catching a couple and moving on, only to come back an hour or so later when I can't get a bite anywhere else. I am getting a little better at slowing down and catching a few extra bass.

TIP

Lightning can strike two or three miles in front of the actual storm.

People are a lot like a school of bass; we're generally around a bunch of other folk. It's a busy school we live in, though, and almost too fast-paced to be gentle and polite. If we will make just two words—"thank you"—the most-used words in our vocabulary, then we'll have a positive effect on everyone around us.

JUNE 26

HAGGAI 1:5

This is what the LORD All-Powerful says:
"Think about what you have done."

KEEPING A LOG can be beneficial to most fishermen. It's particularly helpful if you fish several different bodies of water. I like to record the weather, water conditions, dates, and information on each fish caught. As time goes by, it's amazing how much you learn by reviewing previous trips.

TIP
Fencerows to a bass are like steak bones to a dog.

Most of us are so busy nowadays, we hardly ever examine ourselves. Over time, we can become entirely different people. Tiny changes build up over time like interest on a loan. A little more complaining. A little more gossip, envy, pride, hatefulness. A little more negativity. You get the picture. Take a hard look at who you are today—every attitude, every feeling. What do you see?

June 27

EZEKIEL 16:49

This was the sin of your sister Sodom: She and her daughter were proud and had plenty of food and lived in great comfort, but she did not help the poor and needy.

I'VE HEARD IT a million times: "Oh, what big, fat, beautiful bass!" We like our bass fat and our women skinny. Half of America is on some sort of diet. We live in the most abundant country the world has ever known. With that has come the most pride in the history of mankind. Pride so big it threatens America's very existence. From gay pride to the sociopolitical pride that kicks God out of government and even our homes. Many people have become too proud to be saved by God.

TIP
Willow leaf blades work best when fishing grass.

God destroyed Sodom because her pride and focus on comfort reached the heavens. How high is the pride of Americans piled before the Almighty God—and how long will He wait?

2 PETER 3:8

To the Lord one day is as a thousand years,
and a thousand years is as one day.

MY BUDDY HANK PARKER once told me that what happens today won't matter a thousand years from now. He is right, and I guess if we all took on every day with that attitude we'd be a lot better off.

God probably doesn't wear a watch or even own a calendar. The Bible says He never sleeps, so an alarm clock wouldn't be of much use to Him. Our whole lives here on this earth are just a sigh or just a breath. This lifetime is just a speck in the grand scheme of time. What does matter is that a thousand years from now we'll be alive in either heaven or hell. That's why God doesn't sleep. He's busy raising up preachers, Sunday school teachers, missionaries, singers, musicians, laypeople, your friends, and even you to tell about the good news of Jesus.

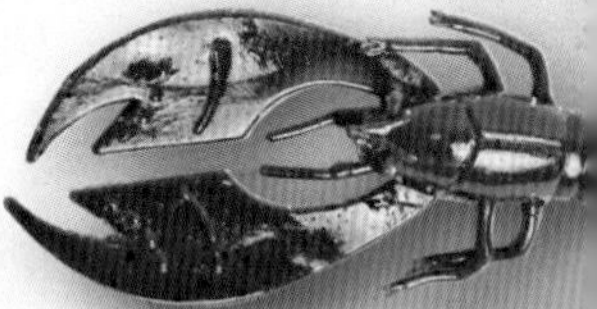

TIP

With a jig or worm, most strikes are on the fall or drop.

June 29

HEBREWS 10:24

Let us think about each other and help each other to show love and do good deeds.

THERE IS AN OLD JOKE about hole-jumpers in tournament fishing—*I guess they thought I needed help on that spot, so they crowded in and helped me fish it.* Obviously, this doesn't help; it hurts fishermen, and it's not at all what God is talking about in today's scripture.

TIP

If the fish are schooling, have several rods rigged with lures that they might bite.

Jesus said that loving and helping others is just about as important as loving God. Why? Because God's whole being is about love and about help. He created Adam and Eve with His love, and He helped them daily. All through the Bible this picture is revealed over and over, especially in the life, death, and resurrection of Jesus—the ultimate expression of God's love and help. Loving and helping others might be just the very best ways to make God smile.

PSALM 33:11

But the LORD's plans will stand forever;
his ideas will last from now on.

AT THE BASS Classic in Charlotte, North Carolina, in 2004, I ran into a longtime, good friend I hadn't seen in a few years—Jon Hall. Jon was an excellent tournament fisherman for many years, but he hadn't competed in a while. Jon told me he had terminal cancer and had come to the Classic to visit with as many of his old friends as he could. It was so good to see him, and it meant a great deal to me that he came by to visit. I knew I may never see him again this side of heaven.

As we grow older, we see more and more of our friends go through these types of problems. We all have a God-appointed day to leave this earth. Praise God that He's already prepared a better place for us to spend forever!

TIP

A small sponge on your jig hook can help hold fish-attractant scent.

July

1 KINGS 3:12–13

I will do what you asked. I will give you wisdom and understanding. . . . I will also give you what you did not ask for: riches and honor.

SOME OF THE BETTER DAYS I've had crappie fishing were days when I actually was bass fishing. Sometime during the day, I'd catch a crappie on a bass lure, pick up a Road Runner, and proceed to catch a livewell full of big slabs. What I'd intended (catching bass) didn't work out too well, but success was supplied in another way (catching crappie). That happens a lot in life too.

TIP
Locate bass with fast-moving crankbaits.

When we pray, God tells us in advance what He wants us to pray for in order to have successful prayers and a full spiritual life. He tells us what He wants to hear! All too often I'm only interested in my needs and intentions, not God's desires. He knows our needs and is ready and able to supply them. What God wants is our hearts.

JUDE 24

God is strong and can help you not to fall.

WHEN GUS RHOTON was ninety-five years old, I took him fishing during summer. The lake was high, and for us to get from our boat back to the dock, we had to walk a warped two-by-twelve plank for about ten feet. When he saw it, he simply and emphatically said no—about three or four times. Finally the rest of us assured him we would wade in the water along both sides and would not let him fall. He walked the plank, got in the boat, and caught several nice bass. Gus told us he didn't get to be ninety-five by being stupid.

TIP

Share a day of fishing with a senior citizen. The blessing will be yours.

We don't need to be stupid about God. He is able to hold us in safety, no matter what the circumstances or how high the water. When we really trust Him completely, God will not let us fall.

JULY 3

REVELATION 3:20

Here I am! I stand at the door and knock.

IT CAN BE all but impossible sometimes to find fish. We've all been there. Sometimes we just run out of options and have no idea where to look next. When we don't get help, those days usually end in total failure. But with just a little tip or two from a friend, we can completely turn that day around.

TIP

For extra color, try a red Daiichi bleeding hook as your trailer hook on spinnerbaits.

When we run out of options with a problem in everyday life, Jesus is that Friend with the solution. No matter how much we have failed in any situation, Jesus can turn it into success. Amazingly, He is always standing there, ready to help, ready to give that victory. He's knocking on the door of our hearts. We just need to open up to Him!

July 4

ROMANS 12:21

Do not let evil defeat you, but defeat evil by doing good.

THE DROP SHOT technique can be dynamite in the hot summer; almost everything about it is advantageous. Just using light line gives us a little help. With the weight on the bottom and the hook tied above the weight, we can really put a lot of action on these tiny, soft plastic baits. The smallness of the lure also is a distinct advantage.

Pretty much every aspect of doing good is positive, and the devil hates when we do it. With so much evil in the world, it's great to know we can defeat evil with good. When we're exhausted and put down by others, our weapon is to pray for them and to do good to them. Evil will be the loser.

TIP

Bumping a stump or log with your spinnerbait often produces a strike.

July 5

2 PETER 2:9

The Lord knows how to save those who serve him when troubles come.

HEAVY RAINS during the summer are rare, but when they happen, they completely change how we go about catching bass. Most summertime bass spend the daylight hours down in deeper water. Heavy rains and rising water will drive these fish to the bank. This is particularly true up in the river areas of a lake. These fish don't have far to go and can get there really quickly when that "new water" starts pouring in.

TIP

An undersized worm hook will cost you missed strikes and lost bass.

Unlike the heavy summer rains, which are rare, troubles will come even to those who serve God. At times, it seems unfair to do God's work and still have problems, but we do. We must remember that we serve a God who has the power to rescue us from whatever trouble we encounter or get ourselves into. For me, I certainly do need lots of God's help.

DEUTERONOMY 26:18

The LORD has said that you are his very own people, . . . But you must obey his commands.

IT'S IMPORTANT to be a member of something—a bass club, BASS, FLW, the Federation. We all want to belong and be a part of something special.

God has called us out as Christians to be His very own. We're set apart to be different from the rest of the world who don't call Jesus the King and Lord of their lives. We're actually members of God's family. Our requirement is to obey Him at all times. Almost all of Christianity can be summed up as *obey God*. This is the single most important element of our relationship with God once we are saved. We obey God for His satisfaction and for our good. Rest assured, God wants only the best for you and me.

TIP

A noisy bait, like a Cordell Hot Spot, will locate suspended smallmouth.

July 7

EPHESIANS 3:20

With God's power working in us, God can do much, much more than anything we can ask or imagine.

IT IS SO FRUSTRATING to not be able to find fish or figure out how to catch them. It is doubly so for those who know a great deal about the game. Quite often, just a little clue from nature or the environment can reveal the problem. Cloud cover, wind, a bass swirling on baitfish, or shad flickering on top can end the frustration if we can put all the variables together.

TIP
Let your worms and tubes fall on slack line.

When we have God in us and working for us, we have His supernatural variables working in us. And because of that, He can accomplish so much more on our behalf. We have a God who will always go the extra mile. He will always strengthen and encourage us just a little bit more. We have a God who sets our goals for us much higher than we set them for ourselves.

July 8

ISAIAH 26:7

The path of life is level for those who are right with God.

Windy days in July and August are a blessing in the South. In fact, if we can just get a little breeze in the dog days of summer, it really makes a difference. Most of the year, though, wind and good fishing don't go hand in hand. We like nice, level water.

God says that if you get right with Him, your path through life will be smooth. Does that mean we'll have no problems, no bumps, no mountains? Of course not! Very few people, if any, will go through life like that. I believe what that promise means is that God will smooth out those bumps and mountains. Reliance on Him and knowing with confidence that He holds my future can flatten even the roughest terrain!

TIP

A rubber frog bait is ideal for heavy vegetation in ponds and lakes.

July 9

HABAKKUK 3:2

Even when you are angry, remember to be kind.

CHRIS HAS ALWAYS SAID, "If Jimmy is mad, ask him for his autograph; he treats nicely everyone he meets." Her observation is humorous, but it has given me some serious food for thought. As usual, she's right. No matter how upset, no matter what my problems, no matter what the situation, I can smile and be nice to a total stranger while at the same time be Mr. Grumpy to someone I love.

God knows things will upset us at times. Even Jesus became angry. God becomes angry. But God wants us to pause and to be kind even when situations upset us. Praise God that He's still kind even when we anger Him!

TIP

A hard bottom generally will show up as a double or triple echo on your locator.

July 10

JOHN 20:31

"These are written so that you may believe that Jesus is the Christ, the Son of God."

STRUCTURE FISHING is one of the keys to summertime bass fishing success. Finding a channel edge, a hump, or a secluded deep water brush pile can be a real bonanza. Trusting your depth finder is a must. Most of us don't really know how these units work or how those tiny little chips inside can give us so much information. Somehow we have faith that what we see is actually a roadbed, bridge, drop off, school of shad, and so on.

TIP

Learn to determine the pattern within a pattern.

Like a depth finder, God gave man His Word to show us that Jesus is indeed the Christ, the Messiah, the powerful and almighty King. God's desire is that we all come to Him through His blessed Son and be saved.

July 11

ROMANS 8:31

If God is for us, no one can defeat us.

DURING OUR Oklahoma Sooner Caravan Bass Tournament on Lake Tenkiller, coaches and players fish with selected local bass anglers in the celebrity competition. Many want to draw me as their partner, because they think they can't lose with me. Of course that's not true, but one year I fished with athletic director Joe Castiglione and defensive back Matt McCoy. Joe and I won the tournament by barely edging out Matt's team, and I received plaques for both first and second places.

TIP

The hotter the weather, the slower I fish a topwater bait.

With God on your team, you'll achieve victory every time. No matter what or who your adversary is, the ultimate victory lies with God. Team up today.

2 TIMOTHY 3:16

All Scripture is inspired by God and is useful for teaching, for showing people what is wrong in their lives, for correcting faults, and for teaching how to live right.

IF YOU COULD GET your hands on the ultimate fish-catching book, what would it be worth to you? Every tip, every trick, every idea, and every technique ever developed. Guaranteed success every time out on the water.

TIP

Stained water farm ponds offer great summertime fishin'.

How about a book that tells you everything you need to know about every situation and encounter in your life? This book is available and was written by the almighty God who hung the moon and stars. He cares for you and me so much that He gave us a handbook to live by. Your marriage, health, family, job, hobbies, relationships, worship, attitudes, even your money—these answers are all in there and more. God created us, and He wants only the very best for all aspects of our lives.

July 13

PSALM 121:3

He who guards you never sleeps.

AT A YOUTH FISHING DAY in South Bend, Indiana, I walked along the shore and visited with the four or five hundred kids fishing. I came upon a little girl lying down, half asleep as her bobber went under. "Wake up, wake up! You've got a fish!" She jumped up, but missed the fish, of course. I told her there's no sleeping in fishing.

TIP

If crawdads are available, fish shallow.

We all fall asleep when we shouldn't, but isn't it comforting to know we have a God who does not sleep. He's on the job at all times. When problems mount and worries soar and you find it impossible to sleep, give everything over to God. He is going to stay awake to guard and solve your problem. There's no need for both of you to stay up.

July 14

JAMES 4:10

Humble yourself in the Lord's presence, and he will honor you.

JUST ABOUT EVERY FISHERMAN has an ego, and we really enjoy it when someone strokes that ego. If no one does, we will do it ourselves. We do this particularly if we are around someone who we believe has more than we do or who might be better than we are.

Of course we all really want to be something special and great, but God tells us simply to be humble in His presence. You see, we can fool the world, but we cannot fool God. He always knows! He knows how pride can hurt us. He knows what a trap it is. He knows what it will cost us and what mistakes it will cause us to make. He knows all, and He sure enough knows how to reward the humble. That's a promise.

TIP

Tungsten slip sinkers penetrate grass better than lead weights do.

July 15

LUKE 15:10

"There is joy in the presence of the angels of God when one sinner changes his heart and life."

DURING THE TWENTY-ONE YEARS of Bass'n Gals, it was exciting to watch the progress of many of the women. Some barely stood a chance of catching a fish in those early days, but they became excellent fisherpersons over the course of time. Their fish-catching ability changed right before our eyes.

TIP

A red crankbait will produce in stained water really well.

When you get saved, God gets excited about seeing changes happen in every aspect of your life, perhaps most importantly in your heart. Your old sinful, sin-loving heart is washed clean. All sins are forgotten, and a new you begins to develop. When you really, really turn it over to God, He will turn your life into a brand-new, exciting adventure.

JULY 16

EPHESIANS 5:21

Yield to obey each other as you would to Christ.

IT'S NO SECRET that my best fishing partner is my beautiful wife, Chris. I've spent literally thousands of hours with her in a boat and am still just as excited about the hours we'll spend fishing together tomorrow. I can't imagine what it would be like to have a non-Christian wife. And I know Chris wouldn't live with a non-Christian husband.

TIP

If you hear thunder within thirty seconds of a lightning strike, seek cover.

When people make a commitment to love, cherish, honor, and obey, it's pretty easy to skim over that "obey" part. I'm not sure it would be possible without mutually yielding to obey. The devil hates this kind of godly marriage. He really deplores our respect of Jesus Christ. Bottom line . . . I guess it's godly to carry out the trash when she asks you to!

July 17

PSALM 85:8

I will listen to God the Lord.

As good as fishing is in the springtime, it's hard for me to totally concentrate on catching fish. Why? Because I'm always listening for a turkey gobble. Most of the time I keep camo attire and a shotgun in the boat. Even if it happens during tournament practice, when a turkey gobbles, I'm outta here! Into the woods!

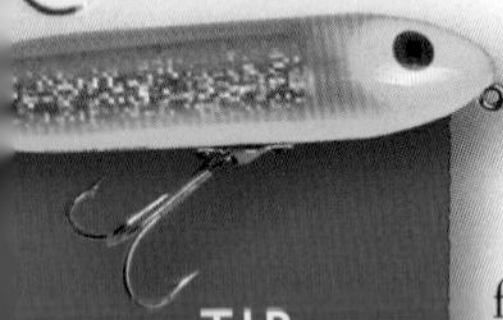

TIP

A color fish locator will make it easier to determine bottom makeup.

It pays to listen just as intently for a word from God. God has the power to communicate with us daily . . . even hourly . . . if we'll but pay attention and listen. He has all the answers, so why not pay attention every minute of every day? It doesn't make much sense to go it alone in even the most trivial matters, let alone in life's major struggles. Make it a priority to listen to God today.

July 18

1 JOHN 2:15

Do not love the world or the things in the world.

WE HAVE THE BEST FISHING in the world here in America, Canada, and Mexico. We are still mostly free to travel between these countries to enjoy that fishing.

We are particularly blessed here in the United States with an abundance of just about everything. Does God want us to enjoy these things? Absolutely! After all, He created all this for mankind to use and have dominion over. What He does require is for us to love Him and never put the world or worldly things above Him. He created this world and all that is in it for our benefit and our pleasure. He created us for His pleasure. We must always keep God first and never, ever put His creation above the Creator.

TIP

Insert a piece of nail into a sinking worm to make it easier to throw in the wind.

MATTHEW 28:20

"Teach them to obey everything that I have taught you, and I will be with you always, even until the end of this age."

I REMEMBER my son, Jamie, and my dad following us out onto Lake Ontario in huge waves. Jamie was driving my Ranger boat even though he was only ten or eleven years old. The waves would almost overwhelm the boat, but Jamie was confident and felt secure. Granddad was beside him, and I was in the boat in front of him watching for any trouble. There was really nothing for him to fear.

TIP

Use a soft plastic jerkbait when bluegill are present in shallow water.

Those who are saved by the blood of Jesus Christ have a Father who will always be there no matter what, even when the storm gets wild and scary. When those we trust fail us, when the devil attacks us, we can count on Jesus. He'll be right there! Always.

JULY 20

MATTHEW 10:39

"Those who try to hold on to their lives will give up true life."

CATFISH ARE INCREDIBLE. They're really a lot of fun to catch and tremendous to eat. The amazing thing to me about catfish is how well they can live out of water. They somehow can hold on for hours and still be just fine when pretty much any other fish would be long gone.

TIP

Baitfish move around more at night.

When Jesus talks about holding on to our lives, He's not talking about breathing. He means clinging to the old sinful life we lived before we met Him. Take a little inventory of the ways you are not Christlike. Anger, greed, lying, stealing, bad attitude, not tithing, pornography, sexual sin—the list could go on and on, but you get the picture. Now, start cleaning house.

July 21

ACTS 10:43

All who believe in Jesus will be forgiven of their sins through Jesus' name.

One of the great things about fishing the Bassmaster Classic is everyone gets a check. We all get paid. We don't have to do anything but qualify for the Classic. We can zero the entire tournament, which some people have done, and still make some pretty good money for the week.

TIP

Try jerking a tube or swimming it for smallmouth bass.

God is an all-inclusive God. He wants no one to go to hell. His desire is that all be saved. He's laid the groundwork for this from the beginning of time. He promised His Son, Jesus, to pay for our sins. How do we qualify for this? Believe in Jesus, whom God sent just as He prophesied for hundreds of years. And here is God's promised paycheck: all sins will be forgiven no matter how many, no matter how terrible, no matter how much trouble they caused. What a God!

DANIEL 1:17

God gave these four young men wisdom and the ability to learn many things that people had written and studied.

Some fishermen have extraordinary ability, while others struggle to catch fish no matter how hard they work at it. Anyone can become better at anything if they work hard, but achieving the top level takes more effort. Quite honestly, being a top fisherman is a gift from God.

I can't sing: I have a lousy voice. I can't dunk a basketball: either I am too short or the goal's too high. I can't do brain surgery: I'm not very smart in that area. But there are many, many things that I can do very well. Why? God's gift to me! God has given each of us some very special talents and abilities. I believe He wants us to use these in the very best ways we can, and He prefers we use our gifts for Him. He probably also wants us to be satisfied with what He's given us.

TIP

Beaver huts extend several feet out under the water.

July 23

1 CORINTHIANS 15:33

Do not be fooled: "Bad friends will ruin good habits."

MOST OF THE TOURNAMENT GUYS have one or two friends with whom they become really tight. They travel together, eat together, room together, and either practice together or at least share information. I've seen both sides of the coin, where this can either help or hurt an individual's chances. Close friendships like this also happen in other activities and aspects of our life.

God doesn't give much leeway here: He pretty much tells us to avoid having bad friends. None of us wants bad friends, but most of us have some who wouldn't rank too high on most folks' lists. I've had enough bad friends to know that you will pay a very high price for poorly chosen relationships nearly every time. God says they will change us for the worse even while He is changing us for the better.

TIP

Search out laydown logs that have a fork in the limbs.

EZEKIEL 7:3

I will judge you for the way you have lived, and I will make you pay for all your actions that I hate.

MOST BASS FISHERMEN dread cold fronts, but a cold front in the summertime usually can make it easier to catch fish. We had a cold front in Oklahoma one summer that dropped the temperatures from 92 to 82 degrees. That ten-degree drop—the cause—gave us the effect of the best shallow water bass fishing since the middle of that spring.

TIP

A bass often hears a spinnerbait or crankbait before seeing it.

Violating God's laws starts a cause-and-effect cycle that will always carry serious consequences. In today's fast-paced, loose-living society, most of what God hates is becoming standard behavior. Lying, cheating, stealing, adultery, blaming others, and doing other such things has become blended into so many lives. Rest assured, no one gets away with sin even though it appears that they are! God is still God, and He's in control.

July 25

ISAIAH 29:18

At that time, the deaf will hear . . . the blind will see.

UNDERWATER ROCK PILES are some of the hottest bass-holding structures you can find. Once summertime hits, you can bet bass will start heading for those rocks. A great technique is a heavy roller jig that you can bounce off the rock pile. This extra noise really helps the fish hone in on your bait.

TIP

Always check to make sure your crankbait is running straight.

As we get older, our ability to hear and see begins to weaken. Isn't it comforting to know that this regression is only temporary and will change in an instant when we die and move on to our eternal reward with Jesus? This old body and these old senses wear out, but God has already designed a heavenly body—a perfect body. Not only for those of us who have used up this body, but for many whose eyes will see and who's ears will hear for the very first time!

July 26

ROMANS 8:35

Can anything separate us from the love Christ has for us?

BASS USUALLY SCHOOL in most lakes in late summer and early fall. It's terrific and fast-paced fishing. Get a good lure into the school, and it's a fish almost every cast. The problem is they don't stay up long. When they go down, it's a waiting game until they resurface. You can always count on a few bass getting separated each time they come up. I usually slow roll a spinnerbait or change to a deep-diving crankbait to pick up a few of these stragglers who've been left behind.

TIP

Avoid the heavy summertime traffic by fishing at night.

We can never be left behind from the love of Jesus. When Jesus stretched out His arms on that cross, He embraced you and me with a love that can't be shaken. Nothing Satan nor his legion of demons can do or lead us into can dampen Christ's love. Trust Jesus: He'll prove true every day.

July 27

ZEPHANIAH 2:7

The Lord their God will pay attention to them
and will make their life good again.

It is frustrating to go those stretches when you can't get a bite. If you fish tournaments, those stretches can quickly turn into the entire day, then two days, then several tournaments.

Life, relationships, and business seem to throw these stretches at us also. The devil has a way of jumping in and piling on. One problem leads to another. Troubles seem to come in bunches and from all directions. When it looks like there's no way out, that's when we need God most, and that's when God is at His best. That is when we don't *need* to pray, we *have* to pray. We don't just read God's Word. We immerse ourselves in it and live in it. I have seen God walk on water many times, and I'm counting on Him to do it again.

TIP

Create your own holes in heavy vegetation to fish later in the day.

July 28

1 PETER 5:8

Control yourselves and be careful! The devil, your enemy, goes around like a roaring lion looking for someone to eat.

YOU'LL CATCH more fish on windy days if you'll use baits you can control in the wind—baits like Hot Spots, Zara Spooks, tungsten spinnerbaits, a tube, or a jig. Those baits cut into the wind. Baits that we can't control create lots of problems.

Not being able to control what we say, do, and think is gunpowder in the devil's barrel. We have so much to guard! We must be very careful with our attitudes, our feelings, and our desires. When you feel yourself losing it, pause and ask yourself who you belong to. If you belong to God, ask Him to come in and take charge. When I give God control of the situation, I have no doubt He will do a much better job with it than I could ever do.

TIP

In general, fish a buzzbait as slowly as possible.

July 29

REVELATION 14:7

Fear God and give him praise, because the time has come for God to judge all people.

BOAT DOCKS are prime for summertime fishing. Bass, bluegill, crappie, catfish—they're all there. Naturally, you can make any dock better by adding a fish feeder, but it also helps to add brush. Cedar or Christmas trees work well, but it's better to use hardwoods because they last longer and are easier to fish. Don't be afraid to hang up in the brush; a few lost lures will be worth the fish you'll catch.

TIP
As bass become inactive, switch to a smaller spinnerbait.

Why should we be afraid of God? He is a loving God, a caring God, a forgiving God. He's also a holy God and will accept nothing less than holiness from those He created in His own image. Can we become holy? Sure—we become holy by trusting Jesus and letting the Holy Spirit do His work in us. With the Lord Jesus, we have nothing to fear and nothing to lose that's worth missing out on Him.

July 30

ROMANS 8:37

But in all these things we are completely victorious through God who showed his love for us.

My decision not to wear a beer patch or place a beer decal on my boat has created some costly problems over the years. Although I lost that battle, maybe I won the war. Now no angler is required to promote beer. It is an option.

Nothing we encounter in life can defeat us if we are saved and belong to Jesus. The full victory we have is eternal life with God. No sickness, no bad relationship, no amount of lost money, no heartbreak, not even death can take this ultimate victory away. God is a mighty, loving God, and He showed us His love in a mighty way by sending Jesus to die on that cross for you and for me.

TIP

Try a white jig in clear water under milfoil or coontail moss.

July 31

MATTHEW 11:28

"Come to me, all of you who are tired and have heavy loads, and I will give you rest."

TIP

Use a Fire Tiger crankbait in muddy water.

MAKING YOUR BAIT run into something is one of the tricks of almost all good fishermen. Letting a spinnerbait, crankbait, jig, worm, or whatever bump a stump, log, or bush doesn't happen by accident. Look for opportunities to create this as much as you can.

Just as good things happen on purpose, it's also no accident when you become weary and seemingly carry the world on your shoulders. The devil is at work every day creating tough situations. Jesus is perfectly capable of handling these trying times. Quite frequently God has provided the solution in advance. We miss this at times until we become so desperate that we finally realize we have only one place to turn, Jesus. Only then do we realize that God was carrying the load all along.

August

August 1

1 CORINTHIANS 6:12

"I am allowed to do all things," but not all things are good for me to do.

When I was a kid working on the dock at Elk Creek on Lake Tenkiller, I always envied the rich kids from the city who seemed to have everything. They had great boats, charged their gas and everything else to Daddy's bill, and generally were allowed to do anything they wanted. I saw all this while I worked at a dollar an hour. I also saw a lot of those kids get into all sorts of trouble.

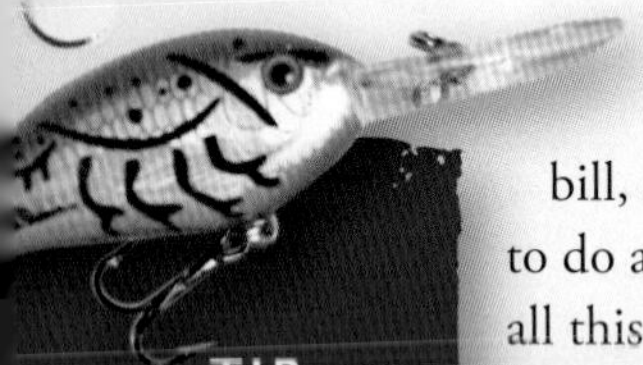

TIP

Bass normally hang around any commercial docks that sell minnows.

Our heavenly Father gives us free will to do all things, but He's also given us His Spirit to guide us and keep us from harming others and ourselves. Pray for His involvement, listen for His guidance, and act upon His advice and leadership.

August 2

TITUS 3:9

Stay away from those who have foolish arguments.

CHRIS'S MOM is over eighty years old (don't tell her I told you this), but she still loves to fish. She still catches her share of bass and catfish, plus more bluegill than anyone. She also loves her God and her church, and she is there helping, working, and worshiping anytime the doors are open. She knows about everything going on at Keys Baptist Church, and the amazing thing is she won't argue about anything with anybody in that church. Chris says her mom just "plays dumb" when someone wants to create a controversy.

Staying out of arguments is probably the smartest thing any church member could do. Let's face it: loving and encouraging one another honors God. Arguing and tearing down is honoring Satan. You make the call.

TIP

Heavy, late afternoon thunderstorms quickly move fish into runoff areas.

August 3

1 TIMOTHY 6:7

We brought nothing into this world,
so we can take nothing out.

ALL TOURNAMENTS start with everyone at zero. We're not handicapped by a scoring system. We all have empty livewells. Within minutes after takeoff, the standings begin to change. We all have the chance throughout the tournament to win or lose.

We're born into this life with nothing, and then within seconds we're wrapped in blankets and we begin to acquire stuff. In the United States, we have the opportunity to acquire staggering amounts of possessions, but at the end of our lives, we all leave with exactly what we started with—nothing. Sure, many people have been buried with mementos, jewelry, prized possessions, even money, but all that stuff remains in that box as we move on. Where we go depends not on what we own, but on who owns us—Jesus or Satan.

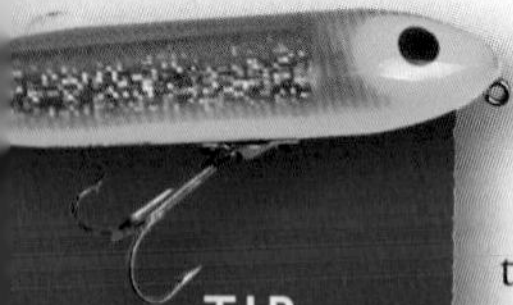

TIP

When you cull during a tournament, mark the next two or three fish you want to cull.

August 4

JEREMIAH 31:3

The Lord appeared to his people and said,
"I love you people with a love that will last forever."

We're financing boats now at Jimmy Houston Marine for either ten years or twelve years. Manufacturers are building boats better than ever now, but you need to take care of one pretty well to make it last that long. The real key is to start out with the best quality boat you can buy. The better the boat, the longer it's likely to last.

God's love for His redeemed is permanent. The quality of His love surpasses anything we can imagine. It's a love I count on every single day. Just about everyone will let us down and disappoint us at some point, but not God. We, too, will at times fail and hurt others, often the people we love most, but God's command to us is to never waver from His love, no matter what.

TIP
Use Reel Magic on your dash and fish locators to keep them looking new.

August 5

1 PETER 5:10

After you suffer for a short time, God, who gives all grace, will make everything right.

ENJOY EVERY DAY you have fishing. Cherish every moment with your family and friends. Live every day in service to your God. We've lost many fishing friends in the past few years to cancer. We have several who are fighting it now. Sugar Ferris of Bass'n Gals penned these words:

Cancer is so limited . . .
It cannot cripple love.
It cannot shatter hope.
It cannot corrode faith.
It cannot eat away peace.
It cannot destroy confidence.
It cannot kill friendship.
It cannot shut out memories.
It cannot silence courage.
It cannot invade the soul.
It cannot reduce eternal life.
It cannot lessen the power of
the Resurrection.

Thank you, Sugar Ferris. Thank You, Jesus!

TIP

Summertime crappie and white bass are active at night using lights under bridges.

PSALM 25:7

Do not remember the sins
and wrong things I did when I was young.

AT PERSONAL APPEARANCES, I like to tease the moms and dads with teenagers. I tell them not to worry about what their sons and daughters will do with the opposite sex; just remember what they did when they were their kids' age. Of course, we all remember how we were less than perfect, and we hope our kids aren't doing some of the same things we did as teenagers.

The truth is, we all sin. If I could live my life over I could write down several pages of sins I would not commit again. Nevertheless, those grievous, foolish, youthful sins cannot be uncommitted. Praise God that through His Son, Jesus, they are forgiven and forgotten by the God who created us.

TIP
A simple change in cloud cover and sunlight may necessitate changing lure colors.

August 7

EPHESIANS 4:2

Always be humble, gentle, and patient, accepting each other in love.

BETTER FISHERMEN learn to adapt to changing conditions. In the South, this can happen several times in a single day, while in California, conditions might not change but once every two or three weeks. Rest assured, though, when conditions change, you'd better have a few tricks up your sleeve.

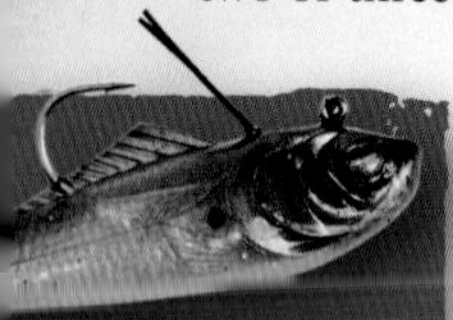

TIP
Remember, crawdads are nocturnal; they move around mostly at night.

One unchanging characteristic of Jesus is He accepts us with love, and He expects us to do the same. Jesus expects us to love not just when others love us, but at all times. When we're hurt, we help. When we're lied to, we tell the truth. When we're cheated, we pay back. When we're hurt, we heal. When we're betrayed, we forgive. Is this easy? Absolutely not! But that's what Jesus did for us.

August 8

EPHESIANS 2:10

God made us to do good works, which God planned in advance for us to live our lives doing.

Today's fishing reels are technical works of art. We've come so far in my lifetime with reels, it's hard to imagine how they could get any better, but somehow they will continue to improve. We started such a simple concept but now actually have computers in our fishing reels. And we've done all of this just to make fishing more pleasurable for you and me.

God is also in the improvement business. He can take a simple saved sinner and transform that person into a mountain of blessing and good to millions. He's done it time after time throughout thousands of years. He saved each individual Christian to do good works. Talk to God today about the good works He has planned for you to do.

TIP

A white blade is more visible on a spinnerbait in murky, muddy water.

August 9

1 CORINTHIANS 6:1

When you have something against another Christian, how can you bring yourself to go before judges who are not right with God?

BEING IN THE BOAT business and fishing on television seem to put a target square on our backs. We've been sued just trying to help a friend sell his boat. Such are the times in America today. We reach out as far as we can to place blame for something on someone else . . . anyone else. It only takes a little nudging from Satan for good people to do bad things.

God, of course, knew this would happen, and He admonished His people to settle their differences among themselves rather than trust the situations to an ungodly judicial system. Christians will often wrong other Christians. God knew this, and He's prepared to get involved in the solutions if we will let Him. After all, God is the ultimate Judge.

TIP

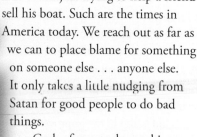

A low stretch line will improve our hookset.

PROVERBS 31:10

It is hard to find a good wife,
because she is worth more than rubies.

MANY A MAN who loves to fish has a wife who doesn't. God's gift to me was not only a wife who loved to fish, but one who is really good at it. Folks all across the country remind me often that she catches more fish than I do. Thanks, but I've been aware of that for a long time.

TIP

It pays to carry a prop wrench and an extra prop.

If you want your wife to become your best fishing partner, make sure she's having fun. Don't kick her out of bed before daylight to accompany you to a lousy fishing hole on a cold, rainy day. Pick out the most beautiful, comfortable day you can and don't go early. Fish the last few hours before sunset. Go to your very best honey hole, fish for whatever is biting, and don't gripe at her, no matter what! Then, let God do the rest.

August 11

MATTHEW 5:44

"But I say to you, love your enemies. Pray for those who hurt you."

When we were building our house on Twin Eagle Lake, we encountered more problems than you could shake a stick at. We faced delays, misinformation, shortages, and all kinds of troubles. I developed calluses that became bigger every day. Many times Chris warned me to forgive anyone who seemed part of the problems, but I really didn't want to. Finally, God used Chris's nudging and convinced me to forgive. When I did, He quickly asked me to pray for the one who hurt me. That was difficult, but I did. Divinely, supernaturally, God healed me and gave me the peace I didn't have. If you're harboring bad feelings toward anyone, pay close attention to Jesus. Forgive. Pray.

TIP

Try drop shotting on those clear, color-bright sunny days.

August 12

PSALM 23:6

Surely your goodness and love will be with me all my life,
and I will live in the house of the Lord forever.

All Chris and I need is an excuse to go to our ranch and lake house. As much as we love beautiful Lake Tenkiller, we love Twin Eagle Ranch even more.

King David's most famous psalm isn't talking about a mere lake house, a country home, a church, a temple, or a mansion. It's talking about living in the very presence of God Almighty. Can we do that? You bet we can. In every situation, in every temptation, in every crisis, His presence is only a whisper away. We only need to call on God, and He's there quicker than a heartbeat. Many times we've blurted out God's name for help in sudden danger. God is on call constantly. The devil wants to come between us, but he can't because God's presence surrounds us at all times.

TIP

Small blades on a larger spinnerbait allow you to fish deeper.

August 13

1 TIMOTHY 6:11

Live in the right way, serve God, have faith, love, patience, and gentleness.

TIP

Follow the morning shade as long as you can.

FISHING INVOLVES so many decisions, especially bass fishing. We make hundreds of decisions every time we go fishing. To catch fish, though, we can base all these decisions on only a handful of criteria.

To live our lives correctly, we need to do only a handful of things. We must serve God, have faith, love, be patient, and be gentle. Can you think of a single time, place, relationship, or activity where these five godly characteristics can fail you? Maybe we should write these characteristics on our calendars, desks, the dashboards of our cars, or even on our tackle boxes. What if we just started this right way of living within our own families and let it blossom from there? Trust me, God would do some mighty things.

August 14

JOHN 9:4

"While it is daytime, we must continue doing the work of the One who sent me".

WITHOUT A DOUBT, fishing is really hard work when it's done correctly. Very few fishermen can put in the five or six long days that tournament guys do every tournament. It is pretty difficult for most anglers to fish really hard and really well throughout the competition.

God, however, is always on the ball, whatever the job, and we need to be working for Him. Maybe His work can be summed up in just a couple of powerful words: *love* and *forgive*. Jesus performed many miracles, preached great sermons, and changed countless lives. Pretty much everything Jesus did, including dying on that cross and rising again, was done to love and to forgive. God asks for exactly the same from you and me. We may never walk on water, but we can love and we can forgive.

TIP

Don't seek safety under trees during a lightning storm.

August 15

MATTHEW 7:17

"Every good tree produces good fruit, but a bad tree produces bad fruit."

ANOTHER OF JIMMY'S rules of thumb: fish the heaviest cover you can find near deep water. Bass get big and mean, but they can be spooked easily. Heavy cover and deep water produce good protection, so that's where you'll most likely find fish.

TIP

Try to determine how fish are positioning on a piece of structure.

In this scripture, Matthew isn't talking about factors that make good fishing; he's warning us about the results of our actions. We must guard what we do. People pay more attention to our actions than our words. They see what we stand for without our telling them. Non-Christians love to see Christians mess up and fail. It's important that our actions match what we say so that, by the power of God's Spirit, we attract others to Jesus.

August 16

ISAIAH 35:2

Everyone will see the glory of the Lord
and the splendor of our God.

THERE ARE SPECTACULAR places to fish around the world. Most of Alaska is like fishing in a picture postcard. There's stunning beauty in just about any direction. I'm told New Zealand and Switzerland are just as breathtaking.

But I'm sure none of these compare to the splendor and glory of the God who made them. The Bible tells us our finite minds can't comprehend God's infinite glory. We also can't comprehend His love, but we can experience it. Through Jesus, God has provided us a ticket into the most glorious kingdom ever—heaven. He has chosen us to be set apart for this glory, this incredible splendor. I'm not too sure what to expect, but I wouldn't miss it for the world.

TIP

Be alert for schooling bass in late summer and early fall.

August 17

1 PETER 5:10

He will make you strong and support you and keep you from falling.

One of the best techniques for fishing standing timber is pitching a worm or tube right at the tree and letting it fall. The trick is to use slack line. Move your rod tip toward the tree to keep your line slack. If the water is deep, peel off line to keep your bait right on that timber.

By giving us free will, God gives us a lot of slack in making choices, good or bad. Do you know people who never seem to fall or make a bad choice, no matter what? They always seem strong and positive no matter how dark the situation. Their secret is living near to God.

Sure, there are times when there seems to be no hope, God then becomes our hope. When we run out of strength, God is our strength. When we have questions, God has the answers. He is our support and He will keep us from falling.

TIP

Search out stumps on the edge of drains.

August 18

MARK 8:36

"It is worthless for them to have the whole world if they lose their souls."

WHAT'S YOUR MOST prized fishing possession? Your Ranger boat, your best Super Caster reel, your boxes full of lures, your fishing trophies and awards? Think about it. What if you could double or triple or have a hundred times more of that prized possession? What kind of price would you pay, and how much effort would you put out to get there? Would you give your soul?

TIP

Pork trailers on jigs and spinnerbaits work better than soft plastics in cold water.

Of course not is what most folks would answer. Yet many have and many more will. We often fail in setting our priorities. Our most prized possession is our soul. It's ours to keep with Jesus or ours to lose to Satan. It's a choice every one of us must make. Most folks already have.

August 19

DEUTERONOMY 28:2

Obey the Lord your God so that all these blessings will come and stay with you.

MANY TIMES in tournaments I've just missed finding a really big bunch of bass. Maybe I was on a spot at the wrong time, didn't go far enough up a creek, or didn't go far enough down the bank. I might have used the wrong lure or technique. I was close, but made mistakes that cost me. Probably every tournament angler can identify with this.

TIP

Feeding periods generally change roughly fifty minutes each day.

I believe that often we come close to God's blessings, but miss out because of things we do or don't do. Not thinking robs us of blessings. Sinning sexually, being greedy, envying, gossiping, telling lies, being proud, and committing other sins short us on God's blessings. God laid out a very well-defined path to receive and keep His blessings. Obey God.

LUKE 12:15

Then Jesus said to them, "Be careful and guard against all kinds of greed. Life is not measured by how much one owns."

CHRIS HAS SAID many times that it's sinful how many fishing lures, worms, and spinnerbaits we have. It scares me to think that Jesus just might agree with her. Perhaps even worse, we still keep getting more.

Jesus was never hung up on stuff. He sent His disciples out to preach with almost nothing but His Word. He wants us to have a relationship with Him and with the Father. He knows what this life is all about.

TIP

Use large willow leaf blades in water with poor visibility.

Two or three times during our forty-five plus years of marriage, Chris and I have come very close to losing everything, and I mean everything. We had accumulated so much stuff, but it was all about to go away. Once we were at peace with losing it all, God stepped in and saved us.

Life is measured by how much God owns us.

August 21

JUDGES 21:25

In those days Israel did not have a king. All the people did whatever seemed right in their own eyes.

AT ANY GIVEN TIME, on any body of water, you can catch fish in a lot of different ways. Almost any lure or technique will work, but obviously some work much better than others. We all fish in what we believe is the right way with the right bait.

Without leadership, people are on their own to determine right and wrong. Without God, what seems to be the right way becomes more perverse, more sinful. Here in America, many things unheard of when I was a kid are now accepted as normal behavior. Some are not only accepted, but are openly rewarded. We make light of sexual sin. Lying, cheating, and greed are open parts of business, and employees believe they have a right to steal. At the same time, Christian values are routinely mocked.

Who's leading your sense of right and wrong?

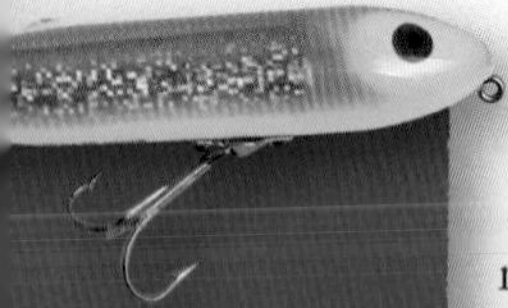

TIP

Use fluorocarbon line in super clear water.

August 22

2 THESSALONIANS 2:7

The secret power of evil is already working in the world, but there is one who is stopping that power.

THERE'VE BEEN many secret lures and techniques to come along over the years. I won the 1986 BASS Angler of the Year primarily on a tandem willow leaf spinnerbait and kept the lure a secret until the first tournament or two. The drop shot, Gitzit, Road Runner, frog, square nose crankbait, Carolina rig, and many, many more techniques were once secrets shared by very few fishermen.

TIP

Use a 1/4-ounce Road Runner head with a Zoom Fluke Jr. for finicky bass.

Here's another secret that needs to be made known: Satan is at work in this world. Some Christians don't even realize how the devil is affecting—or even controlling—their lives. Realize this with all certainty: Satan is real and extremely powerful. So powerful that he will completely destroy you if you are without Jesus Christ.

August 23

1 TIMOTHY 6:9

Those who want to become rich bring temptation to themselves and are caught in a trap.

We get a lot of mail here at *Jimmy Houston Outdoors*. A few times each week, there's a letter about an idea or invention that the sender claims will revolutionalize fishing and make us all rich. Although sometimes we do hear about great ideas and products, most will never make anybody any money.

TIP

When nights begin to cool, morning fishing is better than evening.

Without a doubt, wanting to make more money is tempting, but God tells us it is definitely a trap. I've been in that trap many times myself. Each time, my relationship with God suffered. Each time, I walked head-first into that trap set by Satan. Each time, I failed. God's simple advice is to seek Him first. He will provide everything we need and more.

August 24

JONAH 2:2

When I was in danger,
I called to the LORD,
and he answered me.

EVERYONE LOVES the story about Jonah and the big fish. As kids, we sang songs about Jonah and wondered what it would be like to be fish bait. But what about Jonah? He wasn't too thrilled. In fact, he was downright mad at God about the whole situation. He didn't want to go to Nineveh, he didn't want to preach, he didn't want the people to repent and be saved. He certainly didn't want to be a big topwater plug.

TIP
Always wear a life jacket when the big engine is running.

We all get out of the will of God sometimes. We all disobey God. When we do, trouble and problems are sure to follow. When this happens, we have two choices: we can get mad *at* God, or we can call *on* God for help. Sooner or later, the second choice will become our only option. Better to make it sooner.

August 25

JAMES 4:7

So give yourselves completely to God. Stand against the devil, and the devil will run from you.

EVERY FISHING DAY needs to have a plan. We need to think out in advance how we intend to catch fish. Every tournament fisherman spends a great deal of time on this. Most people modify their plans as the day goes on. Some sell out to their strategies, no matter what.

TIP

Late summer, afternoon thunderstorms can produce some great buzzbait fishing.

If we are really saved, we need to sell out to Jesus all the way. Too many times in too many situations, we turn our backs on God and His principles. When we do, the devil is right there to inflict pain and suffering. Only when we remain totally surrendered to our God can we send the devil packing.

Today, don't play any games with God. Give Him all you've got of yourself, and stand back and see what He can do with you!

August 26

1 THESSALONIANS 5:2

You know very well that the day the Lord comes again will be a surprise, like a thief that comes in the night.

Surprises can be good or bad. We all enjoy the surprise of an unexpected topwater blowup. We hate the surprise of that big fish coming unbuttoned just when we thought we had her hooked really well.

Jesus Christ, my God, is coming back to Earth. That's a fact. The moment He comes will be a surprise to us all. To many, it will be a shock that He showed up at all. To the unsaved, Jesus' Second Coming will be an eternally fatal shock. To those who claim Jesus, He wants to find us loving, forgiving, helping, and telling others about Him. I think if we only knew the time, that is exactly what we would be doing. It could be today.

TIP
Always wet your knot before cinching it down tight.

August 27

ROMANS 10:11

As the Scripture says, "Anyone who trusts in him will never be disappointed."

OUR FISHING EQUIPMENT has become so reliable. I have many reels that are several years old and thousands of hours fishing on them. They still cast and work great, and I trust them in any tournament.

What about people? How many folks do we know who never disappoint us? Not many, if any, but I have a God I can trust in every situation, all the time. He has never let me down before, and He never will in the future. I need Him the most when the people I trust let me down. We will fail and disappoint one another; that is the sin in us. When that happens, run to God as quickly as you can. He is always ready with comfort for your hurts.

TIP

Buy a more powerful trolling motor than you think you will need.

August 28

ROMANS 14:19

So let us try to do what makes peace and helps one another.

As the nights begin to cool, most bass will start to move into shallow water. It is amazing how shallow these bass will roam. I am talking inches of water—not feet. Their primary target is small bluegill and perch. They sometimes literally run the baitfish out onto the bank. Because some of the summer schooling is still intact, these bass roam in bunches and actually help one another trap the bluegill against the shoreline.

Our daily goal should be to constantly help one another. We should help one another for the sake of godliness and not for what we can gain. Just try to imagine what kind of families we could have, what kind of businesses, what kind of churches, if we would all just follow this one bit of godly instruction.

TIP

Muddy springtime rivers turn into great fish-catching color water in late summer.

August 29

MARK 11:25

"When you are praying, if you are angry with someone, forgive him so that your Father in heaven will also forgive your sins."

Some of the best trout-fishing holes in this country are really difficult to reach. I have friends who will hike five or six miles to get to these remote honey holes. I know one person who is hiking fifty miles roundtrip this weekend to catch golden trout, and the top altitude is 13,000 feet. Now that is a difficult fishing trip!

TIP

Try rigging the same crankbait with different line sizes to fish different depths.

An even harder thing to do is pray for someone who has really made you mad or done you wrong, but God says this kind of prayer is a requirement, not an option. Often the person you are praying for continues to do you wrong. My wife prayed for a man one morning, and later that day he sued us. Remember, though, your prayer is as much for your benefit as it for the person you are praying for.

AUGUST 30

2 CHRONICLES 20:15

The battle is not your battle, it is God's.

ONE OF THE BEST ways to get a youngster hooked on fishing is to hook the fish, hand the child the rod, and let him or her battle the fish. Most kids will learn quickly that they are not actually catching the fish, but the important thing is that they are having fun.

TIP

On a really good piece of structure, try several different casting angles.

We all have battles as we go through life. My preacher, Dr. Andy Bowman, says either you've just fought a battle, you are in one now, or one is just about to happen. That pretty much pegs the slip sinker.

We can fight, or we can let God fight. That choice is ours, but it takes a pretty mature Christian to hand the battle over to God. Save yourself some trouble and give your next battle to God right away.

August 31

MATTHEW 14:30

When Peter saw the wind and the waves, he became afraid and began to sink.

THE TRICK TO CASTING accurately is to concentrate on the structure you are trying to throw near, around, or through. Don't fix your eyes on the spot where you want your lure to land; look at what's near that spot.

We all know that Peter began to fail when he looked at the wind and waves (the problem) and took his eyes off Jesus (the Problem Solver). What a great lesson: success with Jesus, failure without Him. That really sums up God's entire plan for mankind. What do you want to accomplish today? Fix your eyes on Jesus. You and I might never walk on water or accomplish the impossible, but then again, with Jesus, we just might!

TIP

If you don't use a fly rod, try fly fishing with a long, light spinning rod.

September

September 1

LUKE 9:41

Jesus answered, "You people have no faith and your lives are all wrong."

GOOD SPAWNING activity every year is essential for our lakes to maintain good fish populations in today's heavily fished waters. Spring rains create the problem. When lakes rise, beds already made are too deep to receive adequate sunlight. Beds built at the highest water levels are killed out when the lake level drops back. Wrong spawning conditions can be devastating.

TIP

Try a Zara Spook over deep water in the fall. Bass will move several feet to get the bait.

Does a wrong level of faith affect the way we live? *Yes*, because we end up placing our confidence and trust in something other than the God we must have faith in. Like water that's too high or too low, our lives will invariably go in the wrong directions. If your life is not heading the way you want it to, check out where your faith is.

September 2

1 CORINTHIANS 7:23

You all were bought at a great price, so do not become slaves of people.

My friend Greg Broom probably has cooked more fish than anyone else I know. He sells a fish batter mix and cooks samples at every Bass Pro Shop opening or event. I guess he has fried literally tons of fish. We recently were talking about *The Passion of the Christ* DVD selling 4.1 million copies in one day. Amazing! Greg said even more amazing was that anyone would go through all that pain and suffering for Greg Broom and for Jimmy Houston. But Jesus did, and realizing that should make us want to please Him in all aspects of our lives.

The things of this world, the sins of this world, the people of this world, have no ownership on born-again Christians. Let's live like it. The price of our sin has been paid in full!

TIP

The more erratic you work your bait, the better.

September 3

DANIEL 9:18

We do not ask these things because we are good; instead, we ask because of your mercy.

My son and I dove hunt every year the first week in September. We have been doing this as long as I can remember. I guess Jamie started going with me when he was seven or eight years old. The amazing thing is we kill a limit every single day we hunt every year. Why? Because we are really good shots? No—because we hunt where there are lots of birds.

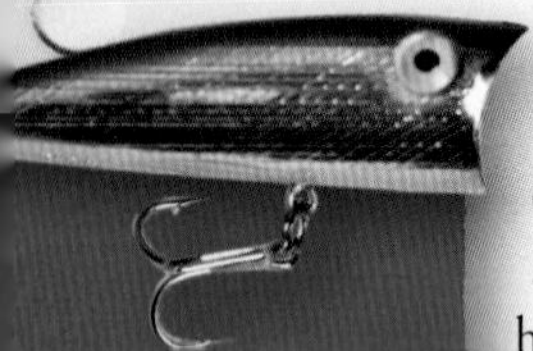

TIP

Watch your locator for a thermocline during the hotter months.

Can we claim blessings and benefits from God because of how good we are? No, our God has lots of mercy. God's goodness—not yours and not mine—is what life is all about. Thankfully, God's goodness and mercy is plenty sufficient. It is all we need in all circumstances. And you can count on that mercy to last throughout eternity.

September 4

PSALM 31:7

I will be glad and rejoice in your love,
because you saw my suffering;
you knew my troubles.

MY GRANDDAUGHTER, Jordyn, is a fish-kissing little rascal. She has been kissing fish since way before she was big enough to actually catch fish. Her favorite? Bass, of course. We were cleaning a few small bass one day to eat, and she had to kiss every one before I filleted it, even though that last kiss might be just a little late to show her love.

God has kissed us with His blessings. He's always standing by to help because He loves us. His love is not based on whether we deserve it or not. In fact, most of the time we don't. He always knows what we are going through and will never let us suffer more than we can bear. Rejoice today. Heavenly help is on the way.

TIP

Try a gold and black Cordell Hot Spot in flats where shad are present.

September 5

ISAIAH 42:21

The Lord made his teachings wonderful,
because he is good.

We study bass fishing because we want to be more successful at catching bass. We watch television shows, read books and magazines, and attend seminars, all to achieve greater success. We assume the teachers are sharing their best information with us.

TIP

Study land contour as you drive down the highway. Imagine it covered with water.

The Bible is the most helpful instruction book ever written. Called the Book of Life, it certainly is that. Life present, life past, life future, and life eternal. Everything God wrote in His Bible is for our good. From our work habits to our eating habits to every relationship we will ever have, God has laid down teachings for our benefit in all situations. We only need to live them.

September 6

LUKE 8:50

"Don't be afraid. Just believe, and your daughter will be well."

MY PREACHER, Andy Bowman, told of an eighty-six-year-old deacon he served with in Florida. This man was saved at age sixty. His wife died when he was seventy, and shortly thereafter, the deacon himself was diagnosed with terminal cancer and given only a few months to live. He told God he was ready to go. But God told this old deacon He still had things for him to do and would cure the cancer. He went back to the doctors and told them he wasn't taking any treatments, because God had said He would cure him. They ran more tests, and sure enough, the cancer was gone.

TIP

Bass will move to the tips of points to feed.

Just like when Jesus walked this earth, God is in the healing business. He asks only that we believe and not be afraid.

SEPTEMBER 7

DEUTERONOMY 31:19

I am offering you life or death, blessings or curses. Now, choose life!

IF YOU GAVE a big old fat bass the choice of hitting a hot skillet or being kissed and released, which do you think she would choose? I am going to bet she'd rather avoid the hot grease no matter how bad a kisser you are. Yet God has given us just that same choice, and many do indeed choose the frying pan. Why is that? Is it too difficult or too simple to believe? It is simple! Do you feel you are not worthy? Well, you're not! Does it cost too much? Jesus has already paid the price—in advance! Do you not have the time for God? Eternity is forever! That fish we hold in our hands is at our mercy for life or death. We are at God's mercy, but unlike that bass, we have a choice.

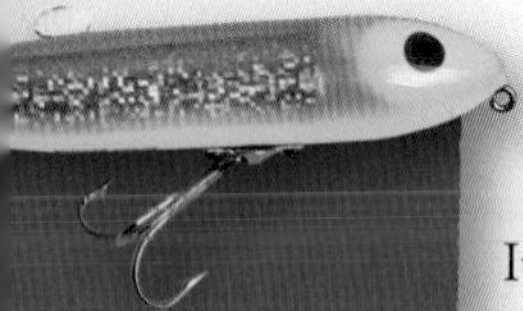

TIP

Only kiss bass of the opposite sex. I never kiss boy bass!

September 8

HABAKKUK 2:4

Those who are right with God will live by faith.

THERE ARE MANY WAYS to fish a Road Runner. All can catch fish. There are really a lot of combinations of Road Runners. I suppose hundreds, when you consider size, color, and type of tail. Any can be right, depending on the situation. Each can also be equally as wrong.

There really is no wrong situation for depending on God to get things right. No illness, no money problem, no hurt relationship, not even death. We are simply to live by trusting Him. Easier said than done? You bet it is, but the only way any of us can experience God's power is by going through some times so tough, we can't handle them alone.

TIP

Never overlook a shady bank, no matter how small the shaded area is.

September 9

REVELATION 3:20

Here I am! I stand at the door and knock.

THIS TIME OF THE YEAR, bass start chasing quite a bit. The fall feed is beginning, and bass are fattening up for the winter. When that old bass chases, he is telling us exactly where he is and what type of lure to catch him on.

TIP

Use deep-diving crankbaits on underwater ledges in late summer and early fall.

For the Christian, Jesus is always telling us how to please Him. No matter where we are or what we are involved in, He will always make sure we hear Him. We can't be in a storm too loud or in a crowd too rowdy for God not to be heard.

We can, of course, ignore Him, and much of the time we do, especially if we are doing something we shouldn't. Rest assured, though, Jesus will speak to us, and we will be a whole lot better off if we will just listen and obey.

EXODUS 23:20

I am sending an angel ahead of you,
who will protect you as you travel.

IF YOU WANT to catch bass on deep structure, find the underwater routes they travel—roadbeds, creek channels, ledges, and edges. Locate their stopping spots, bridges, brush piles, foundations, and the like. Be on that stopping spot when the fish are and—bingo!—you're a hero!

We're a traveling society. I have about two million miles on Delta alone, plus a bunch on other carriers. Probably more prayers are offered up for and by travelers than anyone else. I pray for safety on every flight as well as every trip by land or sea.

Do these prayers work? Of course! I don't know how many angels God has dispatched for my family and me, but it must be a lot. Need an angel today? Ask God. He has plenty.

TIP

Bass will position below undercut banks up river during the summer and fall.

SEPTEMBER 11

ECCLESIASTES 5:18

They should eat and drink and enjoy their work, because the life God has given them on earth is short.

TIM MCGRAW sings a country song about finding out you have a terminal illness. One of the things the lyrics tell you to do is take more time to go fishing. The moral of the song is to live like you are dying. As I grow older, it makes more and more sense to me to make every day special.

On September 11, 2001, nearly three thousand lives ended unexpectedly. I often wonder what each person did the weekend before. How many were saved and are in heaven? How many were lost and will spend eternity in hell? God tells us to enjoy life, enjoy our work, enjoy one another. He knows we will have problems, yet God warns that life is short and to make the most of it. Get out there and make today special for you and for those around you.

TIP

Always experiment with lure speeds.

September 12

COLOSSIANS 4:2

Continue praying, keeping alert,
and always thanking God.

I HAVE TRAVELED BY AIR on September 11th almost every year since 9/11. I really did not give it too much thought except in 2002 when our pilot came on the speakers and asked us to buckle our safety belts and have a moment of silence for the anniversary of the attack.

TIP

Single blade spinnerbaits are easier to fish at deeper depths.

Terrorism is probably here to stay, and Jesus is still the answer. As we pray to Him, we must thank God for keeping us safe while we're on the watch for unusual and suspicious behavior around us. Those of us who fly a lot may have additional responsibilities, but we must always pray, stay alert, and thank God.

SEPTEMBER 13

2 CHRONICLES 20:20

Have faith in the L*ORD your God,*
and you will stand strong.

BUZZBAITS ATTRACT big fish in the fall. You will miss several strikes, and bites may be few and far between, but if you will stick with a buzzbait, especially if you have a little wind or rain, you have a great chance of catching a really big bass.

TIP

There are always fish in shallow water.

Faith in God is what living a Christian life is all about. Like fishing with buzzbait, we will have problems, and at times God's blessings will seem few and far between. But we are guaranteed to catch the big one—heaven! Faith in Jesus gives us the strength to stand firm when everything and everybody around us seem to be crumbling. Faith is our foundation to lean against when we start to topple. If you ask God for anything today, make it a request for more faith.

September 14

MATTHEW 4:17

"Change your hearts and lives, because the kingdom of heaven is near."

THE HURRICANE SEASON plays havoc with the fishing in Florida and all along the East Coast. It also makes a mess of things in Louisiana and Texas at times. The damages far outweigh the benefits, but some changes in land and water can help fishing later on.

As Christians, we know that whatever storms hit us in life, there's a big benefit coming later—heaven! If we positively knew Jesus were coming back tomorrow or next week or next month, how would we feel and act? What would you and I do differently? How would we rearrange our schedules, our priorities? The truth is, Jesus just might come back tomorrow, and He warns that our hearts and our lives need changing. Where can we start? The first place might just need to be our relationship with Jesus Himself.

TIP

Use a shad-colored crankbait if the current is flowing.

SEPTEMBER 15

LUKE 9:13

We have only five loaves of bread and two fish, unless we go buy food for all these people.

WHEN YOU LOOK at some of today's fishing heroes on television, you see tremendous fishermen with celebrity status and great influence. Early on, though, they were something considerably other than superstars. Bill Dance was a furniture salesman, Roland Martin was a fishing guide, and my friend Hank Parker was somewhat of a hippie. (God did clean him up pretty good, though.) God has the power to make a lot out of a little.

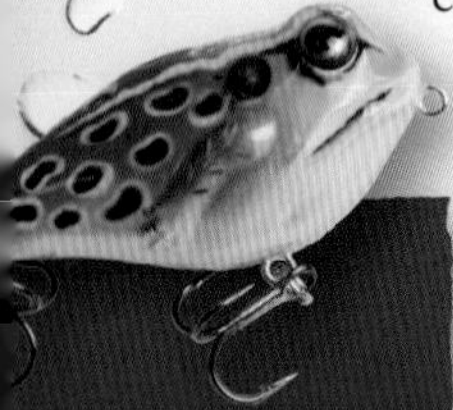

TIP

In deep water, if your line stops falling, set the hook.

If Jesus can feed five thousand men with a couple of tilapia and five biscuits, what can He accomplish with you and me? Whatever circumstances you are in, whatever your dreams and goals are, never ever leave Jesus out for a single moment. He has the ability to turn you into a tremendous person.

ROMANS 9:24

We are those people whom God called.

MANY OF THE TOURNAMENT GUYS call local tournament fishermen to learn about lakes with which they're not familiar. Most locals are really excited when a big name pro calls them for help.

If you are looking for something to really get excited about, think about who called you to be a Christian. Who chose you to be one of His? No one less than the God who created the world. If you get to feeling your life is falling apart, that no one loves you, and no one cares, remember whose family you belong to. Would you get excited if Roland Martin, Larry Nixon, or Woo Daves called? This is infinitely better. Start jumping for joy! God Himself has called!

TIP

A slider head jig will give a worm more action than a slip sinker.

SEPTEMBER 17

PSALM 11:5

The LORD tests those who do right.

IN ORDER TO FISH professional bass tournaments, all you need to do is pay an entry fee. In order to fish at the highest level of BASS or FLW, you must qualify. You are tested at the lower levels before you can play with the big boys.

We don't have to pass any test to become a Christian, but once we join up, we are tested often. We are tested in order to be molded into the kind of Christians God wants us to be. God doesn't need namby-pamby Christians. He wants and uses Christians who have been tested by whatever life can throw at us. We're forged into Christians who have patience, perseverance, humility, forgiveness, generosity, and gratefulness. Mature Christians are tough and know how powerful our God really is.

TIP

If you fish from the bank, use a Smartcast wireless fish finder.

PROVERBS 28:10

Those who lead good people to do wrong
will be ruined by their own evil,
but the innocent will be rewarded with good things.

PONDS REACT the same in the fall as in the spring. Fishing improves more quickly in ponds in the spring, because the water warms up earlier than in larger lakes. Reverse that in the fall: that's right, water in ponds will cool more quickly. This sets off an early fall feeding frenzy.

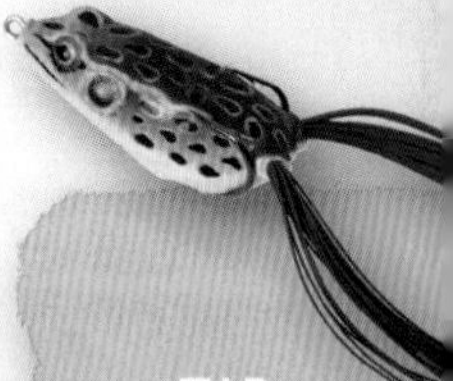

TIP

Pay close attention to the small details in fishing.

The Bible tells us to choose our friends carefully. The smaller our faith is, the more quickly it will be warmed or cooled by the good or bad people we're around. God knows that one bad apple can ruin the barrel and that one evil person can certainly lead many Christians astray. We need to be on the lookout for the devil masquerading as a friend when he is actually determined to lead us into trouble.

SEPTEMBER 19

LUKE 12:58

"If your enemy is taking you to court, try hard to settle it on the way."

IT IS PRETTY COMMON KNOWLEDGE that I intended to be a lawyer. One of my college degrees is in political science. I have said many times that God saved me from being a lawyer. Praise God, He made me into a fisherman and let me make a living at a really super-fun job.

TIP
Sweep your rod when casting a Carolina rig.

Jesus knew long ago how messed up the legal system would become. He knew the greed of man would turn the justice system into a money-bent paper chase. He knew about frivolous lawsuits and the desire of mankind to blame others. But He also gave us some great advice that doesn't cost us $500 per hour.

Do we need to get rid of all the lawyers as Shakespeare suggested? Probably. Must we follow the advice of Jesus? Absolutely!

September 20

James 1:2–3

When you have many kinds of troubles, you should be full of joy, because you know that these troubles test your faith, and this will give you patience.

Rubber frogs have been used for years around heavy grass and lily pads. The Snag-proof frog has been the most popular, but now Yum, Zoom, and others make some great imitation frogs. The trend also has changed as to where to fish these baits. We now fish them just about everywhere—around docks, brush, rocks, stumps, logs, you name it! One thing remains the same, though: to be successful fishing a frog, you must be patient.

TIP

Experiment with new techniques when you are not under pressure to catch fish.

Does God really want us to have real joy everywhere—in troubles, around hurtful people, off by ourselves? Yes, He does! God is a creator, and He is continually at work in us creating someone better. It's not easy to choose joy during difficult times, but I can attest to the fact that it is worth it.

SEPTEMBER 21

MATTHEW 5:6

"They are blessed who hunger and thirst after justice,
for they will be satisfied."

IT MIGHT BE IMPOSSIBLE to satisfy a largemouth bass. They can eat so much that they keep on feeding even when their bellies are bulging. Thank goodness they don't have to be hungry to strike a lure.

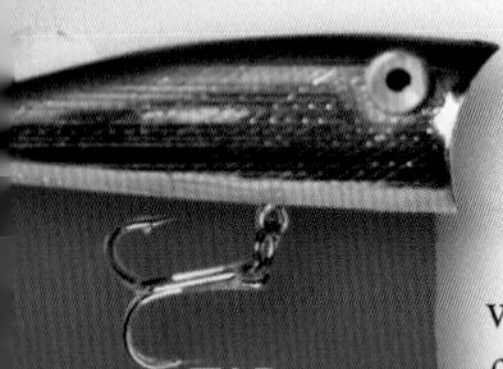

TIP

A high-speed reel will allow you to slam a crankbait into underwater cover.

Being satisfied is something we all want. We desire to be satisfied with our families, marriages, jobs, friends, churches, but complete satisfaction comes only from God. All else will leave us empty and wanting more. God's rule is that our desire must be to do what is right, and He will satisfy us because of that desire. Does this mean He will give us everything we think we need? I don't think so! It does mean that He can enable us to be satisfied with whatever we have.

September 22

PROVERBS 28:25

A greedy person causes trouble,
but the one who trusts the Lord will succeed.

One of the best places to find a school of bass this time of year is on a ledge, creek channel, or point. Bass school on these spots to feed when shad get active. If you can get one bass to bite, the others often will get greedy and go into a feeding frenzy. Great for you; trouble for the bass.

TIP

Shad will get active on manmade lakes when current begins to flow.

Greed is difficult for most of us. There's a fuzzy line between greed and ambition. We all want success, and often success and greed are measured by what we have. I believe greed is actually measured by what it costs you, not by what you have. Greed is what you are willing to pay (or give up) to get what you want. God says that success comes from trusting Him. Oh, how simple!

SEPTEMBER 23

HAGGAI 1:13

Haggai, the LORD's messenger, gave the LORD's message to the people, saying, "The LORD says 'I am with you.'"

MY CAMERAMAN Pat Turner, who runs our production company, gets lost on just about every lake we fish. If I ever die out there, and I just might on a really great strike, Pat probably won't find his way back to the ramp. He faces backward when we are running the boat, and he is looking through the camera lens while we are fishing. He doesn't worry about where we are, because he is sure I can always find my way back.

When we belong to Jesus, we never need to worry about being lost or being alone. In the deepest, darkest night, or in our most desolate or trying situation, the Lord promises, "I am with you." It doesn't take long after you are saved to realize just how important and comforting God's presence really is.

TIP

Use a Fire Tiger Hot Spot where muddy water mixes with clear water.

SEPTEMBER 24

ISAIAH 43:4

You are precious to me . . .
I give you honor and love you.

IF YOU ARE A BEGINNING FISHERMAN, or if you are teaching someone to fish, don't dwell on what you are doing wrong. At the same time, be sure to learn from your mistakes. If there is a fisherman out there who doesn't make mistakes, I've never been in the boat with him or her.

TIP

When willow bushes get flooded, break out your spinnerbaits, no matter what time of year.

God knows that we make mistakes in our relationships with Him and with others. He knows we sin even after we are saved. We know, however, that He loves us and that we are more than just important to Him—we are precious to Him. We all want to be loved. We want to be special to someone. How humbling and yet how incredible it is to know that we are very special and loved so very much by the God of the universe. He said so Himself.

September 25

LUKE 7:50

Jesus said to the woman, "Because you believed, you are saved from your sins. Go in peace."

When the bite gets really tough, what is the best tool you have? Whether you go to light-line and small finesse baits or your heaviest flippin' stick in the densest cover available, your best tool is . . . *concentration*. You must really believe you will get a bite on the next cast.

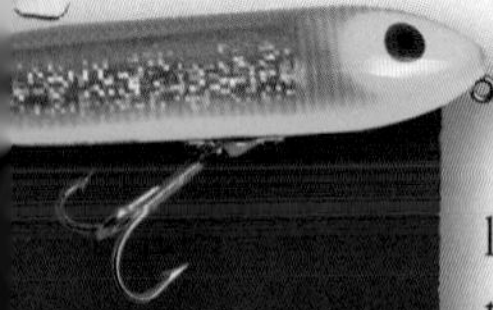

TIP
Visualize how your lure is working under the water.

Believing that Jesus is the Son of God, that He died on the cross for your sins and rosc again to life and is living in heaven now, is the most important belief you will ever have. Concentrate on Him. You have a choice, and no one can make it for you—not your mom or dad, your spouse, or your preacher. This is between you and Jesus. He paid the price and is holding out that nail-scarred hand. Just take hold and believe.

1 CORINTHIANS 4:13

When they tell evil lies about us, we speak nice words about them.

THE CHANGING OF A SEASON is always exciting for fishermen. The fall is particularly exciting because it leaves behind those dog days of summer. As we watch the water temperature drop, we see our success ratios go up. The fall also brings the political season or, as some people call it, the lying season. I am shocked at how easily most people lie. It's like people think God has removed telling lies from His top ten list of sins.

TIP
Don't be afraid to cast deep and bring your bait shallow.

Today's verse really caught me by surprise, and I have had the chance to put it into practice several times recently. As you might suspect, the benefit has been mine. I cannot tell if my saying nice words has had any effect on the ones doing the lying, but it has given me some peace. Try it yourself and let me know.

SEPTEMBER 27

PHILIPPIANS 4:12

I know how to live when I am poor, and I know how to live when I have plenty. I have learned the secret of being happy at any time in everything that happens.

MOST OF THE NEW BREED of bass tournament fishermen operate under the belief that things will change every day. To be successful, you must learn to adapt to the changes. Start with a plan, but realize that the key to each day's success is a moving target.

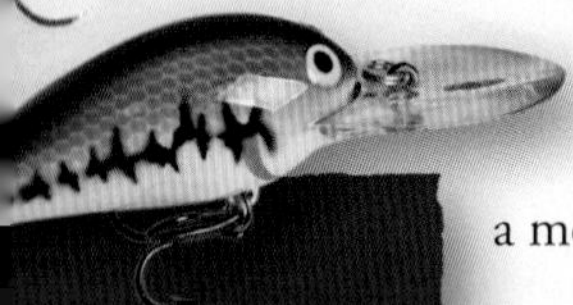

TIP

Reeds close to the deeper water will produce bigger bass.

The apostle Paul knew the key to happiness in everything—whether he was rich or poor, free or imprisoned, hungry or full, beaten or praised. He had learned the secret. That secret for Paul was Jesus. That secret is there for us too. Paul got his strength from Jesus and knew that with Christ his joy was not in physical being or circumstance. His joy was Jesus Himself. All else really pales in comparison, whether it is the most wonderful thing we can imagine or life's most dire circumstance.

SEPTEMBER 28

JOHN 16:24

"Ask and you will receive, so that your joy will be the fullest possible joy."

WHY DO WE SPEND so much time helping others learn how to catch fish? Why are we so patient and understanding with our wives and kids in that teaching process? Why do we take a friend fishing who really doesn't know how to fish? We do these things so that those we love can experience the same joy in fishing that we do.

TIP

Stop or pause a frog in any hole or opening in lily pads.

That is exactly why Jesus is so willing to give to us. He is willing to give whatever it takes so we can experience the joy He has in heaven. It is a joy that we cannot even comprehend—the fullest possible joy. He is also concerned about the daily joy we have in our short time here on Earth. He gave us His Word to make sure we can find that joy, no matter what.

September 29

MATTHEW 5:12

"Rejoice and be glad, because you have a great reward waiting for you in heaven."

HAPPINESS IS a ten-pounder! Yes, indeed. In fact, for me, it doesn't need to be nearly that large to put a big smile on my face (and a pucker on my lips). I have heard so many fish stories, and most end with *I finally caught that really big fish, a fish of a lifetime.*

TIP

Troll points with a Hot Spot or deep-diving crankbait to locate fish.

What God has waiting for us should keep our bobber of happiness and joy floating high at all times. Jesus says it is a great reward, and He should know. He came from heaven and is there right now waiting for us to show up. He told us this in advance so we would have something to really look forward to when times get tough. When your bobber starts to sink a little, set the hook and think about that reward Jesus has waiting.

SEPTEMBER 30

PSALM 34:19

People who do what is right may have many problems, but the LORD will solve them all.

WHEN I THINK BACK to the early days of tournament fishing for Chris and me, it seemed like life was a constant struggle—raising two babies, starting a career, paying bills, and playing in this new deal called bass tournaments. All the while, we were trying to develop a strong relationship with each other and with the God we both trusted so much. I never thought I would say it, but indeed, those were the "good old days."

TIP

Bass normally suspend in cover and not on the bottom.

Now our struggles include several businesses with more than a hundred people working who need a regular paycheck. We deal with bankers, lawyers, customers, suppliers, sponsors, friends, and even a few enemies. Most people are really a blessing. The God whom Chris and I trusted as teenage newlyweds is still right there solving our problems, one by one, and our trust in Him is even greater now.

October

October 1

LUKE 19:10

"The Son of Man came to find lost people and save them."

How do you find a bass that weighs only a few pounds in a body of water that covers thousands of acres? You learn to go where that bass lives.

Where did Jesus look to find sinners needing to be saved? He went where they lived. Praise God, He came looking for me.

TIP

The older and trashier a boat dock is, the better it is for fishing.

It is surprising to think Jesus would leave heaven for any reason. It is even more astounding that He came here to be rejected, humiliated, beaten, and crucified just to pay the price for the sins He knew I would commit. Would you leave your home to pay for a murder someone else committed? Would you suffer beatings for lies you didn't tell? How about letting nails be driven into your hands for adultery you had no part of? Well that is what Jesus did—a billion times over.

October 2

ISAIAH 33:6

He will be your safety.
He is full of salvation, wisdom, and knowledge.
Respect for the Lord is the greatest treasure.

Chris and I have been caught in many storms, many times, on many lakes. When I think back, we have outlived several cats with their nine lives. Yes, we have had some close calls and sure, we were scared, but our God has always been our Safety. God is so awesome, and He deserves and commands our respect in every way possible.

This respect is not for God's benefit; it is for ours. Only when we store up this respect can we fully experience His wisdom and His knowledge. True wisdom and knowledge come only from God.

TIP

Picture in your mind how a bass is positioned on a piece of cover.

Try adding a request for wisdom and knowledge to every prayer. Give God a chance to let these grow in you. As they do, your treasure chest of respect for God will become even fuller.

October 3

PROVERBS 22:4

Respecting the LORD *and not being proud will bring you wealth, honor, and life.*

WE PARTICIPATE in many events for kids, and it is always a thrill to see youngsters catch a fish, especially if it is their first fish. They beam all over, and their mom and dad are so proud of them. So when does excitement about that accomplishment turn into pride, and why is pride bad? God says pride is bad and can rob us of so much He wants us to have.

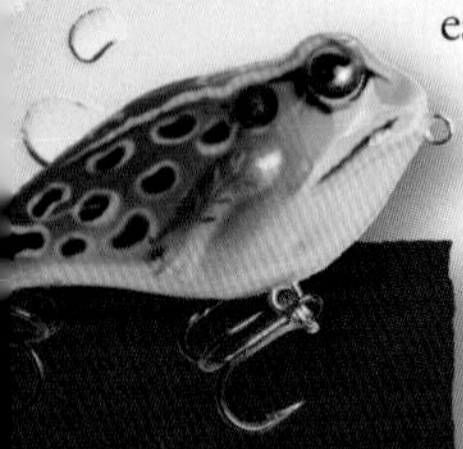

TIP

Big bass are lazy. Use big, slow-moving lures to catch these hawgs.

I believe pride comes when we think we are better than someone else. That is not God's way. Our example is Jesus. He served and honored others. He serves and honors you and me every day. We need to think of others as more important than ourselves. Wouldn't it be wonderful if we Christians would think of one another this way?

October 4

ISAIAH 40:28

The Lord is the God who lives forever,
who created all the world.

When bass are holding tight to cover, we want to fish great target baits like jigs, worms, and spinnerbaits. During the fall, with cooler water, bass start to roam. Very similar to what I use in February and March, a Cordell Hot Spot becomes my favorite bait. I still throw at the bank, make a lot of casts, and cover a lot of water. The fish will be scattered and not holding around structure.

TIP
Learn to half-step a Zara Spook.

God created a changing world, yet God never changes. There is precious little that we can count on in this life, but we can always count on God in all seasons, all situations. The God who created us will never die, and He has promised that we will live forever with Him. I'll take that deal!

October 5

2 CORINTHIANS 5:21

Christ had no sin, but God made him become sin so that in Christ we could become right with God.

Ron Linder, Al's brother, is one of the nicest guys I know. He is also a strong Christian and shares his faith on a regular basis. Ron and Al are so different. Ron is a tough (but gentle) guy whom you would want on your side if a fight broke out. Al is the polished, ever-smiling, fast-talking TV fisherman whom we all love. Together, they became some of the most successful fishermen ever.

TIP

Replace any negative fishing thoughts with positive thoughts.

God has used their differences and different personalities for their benefit. He also has made them the same to Him through their faith and belief in Jesus. God sees us all as saved sinners because of Jesus. Nothing else—and I mean nothing else—really matters.

GALATIANS 5:22–23

The Spirit produces the fruit of love, joy, peace, patience, kindness, goodness, faithfulness, gentleness, self-control.

WE GET TO TAKE A LOT of people fishing—kids, older people, celebrities, politicians, singers, CEOs, preachers, people from all walks of life—and my primary goal is to make sure they have fun. My job is a piece of cake because of what God's Holy Spirit has given me. Looking at each fruit of the Spirit, I see how each plays a major role in fishing with someone, often someone I have met for the very first time.

Study this fruit and see how important they are in your relationships with your spouse, your children, your boss, your employees, your enemies, and even people you meet for the first time today. Jesus promises eternity, but He gives you the tools to live great day by day.

TIP

Transition fishing line (that changes color) will help you catch more fish.

October 7

EPHESIANS 6:12

Our fight is not against people on earth, but against the rulers and authorities and the powers of this world's darkness, against the spiritual powers of evil in the heavenly world.

FISHING IS SOMETIMES more about fighting the natural elements rather than figuring out the fish. This is especially true in tournament fishing where we must compete no matter what the conditions. Often, if we can overcome the bad weather, changing water conditions, or other circumstances, we can succeed.

TIP

Crappie begin to move shallow again at this time of year.

Many of the struggles and problems we face in life come with great battles. But what are we really fighting? Bad personal relationships, money problems, coworkers, companies, lawsuits? According to God, our adversary is none of the above. It is the devil himself and his legion of demon angels. Do we have the strength, power, or ability to fight this battle ourselves? I think not, but I know One who does, and His name is Jesus!

ECCLESIASTES 7:29

God made people good,
but they have found all kinds of ways to be bad.

DURING THIS TIME OF THE YEAR, a lot of our lakes have what we call "glop" on them. This glop forms a solid surface in shallow water and around docks, laydowns, and stumps. I like to fish a spoon on top of this glop. The spoon leaves a trail so you can actually see what you have fished. Bass miss the spoon often and leave a hole in the glop. Have a worm or jig handy to throw in that hole, and it is generally a sure fish every time.

TIP

The strike zone of a bass enlarges as a weather front approaches. Use faster moving lures.

Like that bass strike messes up the top of the glop, we all find ways to mess up God's good creation—us! We sin, no matter how hard we try not to, or how holy and righteous we think we are. We are so fortunate to serve a God who sent Jesus to pay for our mess.

October 9

PROVERBS 16:24

Pleasant words are like a honeycomb,
making people happy and healthy.

ONE OF THE KEY THINGS to remember about a brush pile is that the brush usually spreads farther around down there than you think. After you have fished a brush pile—not before—spend several minutes perusing the pile with your fish locator. See if you have any brush sticking out the side or maybe another good piece of brush close to the main pile.

TIP

Learn to read and interpret topographical maps.

Pleasant, kind, and happy-sounding words also go a lot further than you can ever imagine. What would your words be if Jesus Himself walked into the room? I know my countenance would brighten in a heartbeat no matter how bad my day was or how big my problems seemed. Well, He *is* in the room right now.

October 10

JOSHUA 1:9

Don't be afraid, because the Lord your God will be with you everywhere you go.

DURING A TOURNAMENT practice on Lake Russell in Georgia, Chris and I had caught several good bass up to seven pounds on a couple of bridge crossings. We caught these fish buzzin' a spinnerbait just a few inches below the surface. During the tournament this didn't work at all. I started slowing down my bait until I was literally crawling that spinnerbait along the bottom. Bang! The fish finally bit the bait. I caught a great limit every day. I didn't need to run all over the lake. The fish were there all along, and I just needed to adjust to them.

Jesus is always right there with us, no matter what changes around us. We must not fear. God will provide, and He is anxious to do so. We just might need to adjust our attitude a bit.

TIP

Fish both the outside and inside edges of weed beds.

October 11

MATTHEW 13:50

"The angels will throw the evil people into the blazing furnace, where people will cry and grind their teeth with pain."

Homer Circle, the legendary outdoor writer, penned a prayer that ends with him asking to be judged big enough to keep. Ron Linder talks about being scooped up by the gentle net of God's grace. Every Christian should unquestionably understand that God practices "catch and keep," not "catch and release." Irrespective of what God is doing in your life or mine, the key reason to be saved is to keep from being thrown into hell. Heaven and hell are not states of mind; they are very real places. Heaven is as good as good could ever be, and hell is as bad as bad gets. We each have an appointed time to die and leave this earth. We will spend eternity somewhere. I choose heaven; I choose Jesus.

TIP

My favorite jig color is a black/blue/purple combination.

OCTOBER 12

PHILIPPIANS 4:19

My God will use his wonderful riches in Christ Jesus to give you everything you need.

ROCKS AND ROCK PILES can be great places to fish, especially if you have a lake that has few rocks. Those occasional rocky spots can really be hot spots. But lakes with rocks and rocky banks and ledges everywhere can be tough. In fact, on such lakes I concentrate on non rocky cover, like docks or wood. By the way, a Cordell Hot Spot is a super bait to fish on rocks.

There will always be rocky times in everyone's life. God knows this, and we might as well accept it. The key is that God knows exactly what we need to get through these times, and He has promised to supply what we need, even if it's not all that we want. Look back at some of your rockiest times and remember how God gave you exactly what you needed to make it across those rocks.

TIP

Have a worm handy to follow up missed strikes on topwater baits.

October 13

MATTHEW 16:18

"On this rock I will build my church, and the power of death will not be able to defeat it."

SMALLMOUTH FISHING in the Great Lakes and upper Northeast can get really easy if you can locate isolated rocks. A decent-sized rock will hold a smallmouth or two under just about any conditions. Good polarized sunglasses are a must. Try to fish the shady or undercut side of the rock, if possible.

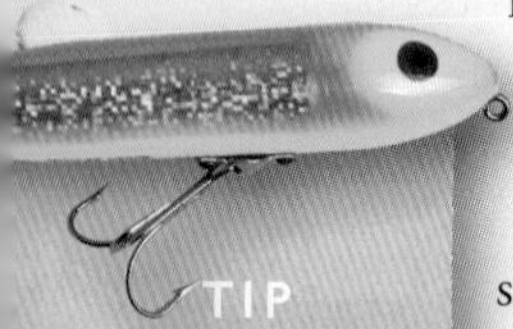

TIP

Engage your reel on a buzzbait the instant the lure hits the water.

When Jesus told Peter He would build His church on a rock, He wasn't calling Peter that rock, even though the name *Peter* means "rock." The rock Jesus would build on was His death, burial, and resurrection to conquer sin.

The church is not made up of buildings, but of people believing in the gospel. Without that rock of Jesus' resurrection from death, there would not be a church. Is Jesus building in you, or are you just warming a pew?

OCTOBER 14

JOHN 8:11

"I also don't judge you guilty. You may go now, but don't sin anymore."

AROUND THE TOURNAMENT weigh-in sites, we have off-limits areas where we are not allowed to fish. There are probably more daily disqualifications for this rule violation than all other rules combined. It is pretty cut and dried; you are either guilty or you're not! It is usually an honest mistake or, at the very worst, a dumb mistake. No one fishes the off-limit release areas intentionally to cheat. They are just mixed up as to where the boundaries are.

TIP

A bone-colored crankbait with an orange belly works well in muddy water.

Sin is sin, whether committed on purpose or unintentionally. All sin must be paid for or punished. That punishment is eternal separation from God. Praise God, He sent Jesus to pay the price so we can avoid the punishment for going outside God's boundaries. Jesus says, "I don't judge you guilty." For this, we certainly should sin no more.

October 15

ISAIAH 13:11

The Lord says, "I will punish the world for its evil and wicked people for their sins."

Fall fishing is fantastic pretty much all over the country. As the water cools down, shad move into creeks, and bass and crappie get really active on points. It is also a time of great changes in weather—severe weather like tornadoes and hurricanes, lightning fires, floods, and drought. The 2004 hurricane season was one of the worst ever for America. Is God trying to tell us something? Is what's happening all around us a warning that this country needs to come back to God? If so, it doesn't appear we are paying too much attention to those warnings.

TIP

Bass in clear water rely more on sight and can see lures more than thirty feet away.

Most people didn't listen to what God was telling them through Isaiah either, but everything God warned about happened. God is true to His word. America must change in order to continue to exist.

OCTOBER 16

JEREMIAH 15:11

The LORD said,
"I have saved you for a good reason."

CLEAR WATER is pretty much defined as being water that allows you to see a white lure down four feet deep or more. The combination of clear water and cooling temperatures is great to fish large-bladed spinnerbaits. I like a half-ounce Booyah with tandem willow leaf blades. Best skirt colors are chartreuse and white and perch color. Bulge the water with the big blade and get ready for some killer strikes. This combination works because bass have adapted to the clear water.

We are saved by God because He has a clear purpose for our lives. I believe God has a purpose for each of us *every day*. How disappointed He must be when we fail to recognize the opportunities He gives us. What purpose does God have for you today?

TIP

Slow down and concentrate on where you want your lure to land and how you want it to work.

OCTOBER 17

HEBREWS 12:4

You are struggling against sin, but your struggles have not yet caused you to be killed.

MUDDY WATER is a struggle for many fishermen, especially those who are not used to it. Anglers who fish primarily clear lakes are often stymied when water looks like a Yoo-Hoo drink. Here in Oklahoma and those states around us, we thrive on muddy water. Bass are more object-oriented. Slow down with jigs and spinnerbaits, put those lures in the heaviest cover you can find, and muddy water will get a whole lot easier.

TIP

In the fall, the most important thing to a bass is food.

Most of us struggle to be the Christians we want to be. We fight against the mud of anger, harsh words, envy, jealousy, greed, slander—and this list merely scratches the surface of our list of personal sin. This struggle is daily and difficult, but it is a battle God wants us to fight. So, by His grace, we can be better Christians down the road.

October 18

PSALM 128:1

Happy are those who respect the Lord and obey him.

I HAVE MANY RULES OF THUMB in fishing. These are rules I follow wherever we are fishing. One simple rule is, bigger baits catch bigger bass. Another rule is to fish a spinnerbait at a depth just before it goes out of sight.

You need to have your very own set of "rules" to fish by. They can be quite a bit different from mine, but they must have a foundation of facts and experience. Follow those rules and you'll catch more fish.

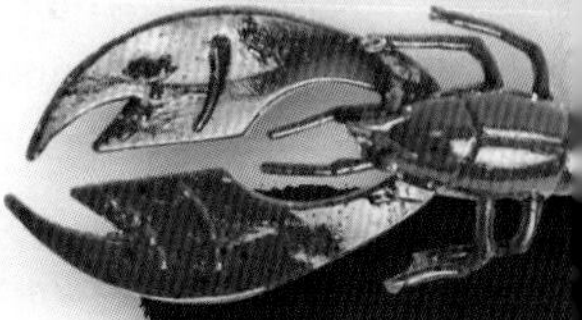

TIP

Use a 36-volt trolling motor if you want to cover a lot of water.

Although the Bible is more than a book of rules, God has given us commands and instructions in it that we must follow to be happy. My rules of thumb help me catch more fish. God's rules of thumb are designed to give us a fuller, richer, more complete life.

October 19

JOB 36:22

God is great and powerful;
no other teacher is like him.

I USE A STRONG 24-VOLT Minn Kota Trolling motor on my Tracker boats and a super-powerful 36-volt on my Rangers. I use the strongest trolling motors that Minn Kota makes, over one hundred pounds of thrust. I always want the most powerful, with the very best batteries, so I can fish under any conditions and can stay on that trolling motor all day. I demand the very best, even though I need all that power only during a small part of my fishing day.

I also serve a mighty, powerful God. He is a God so great that no matter how difficult the conditions become, He can plow right through them. I might not need all of God's power every day, but it is always available and just waiting to be loosed.

TIP

Search out areas that have both deep and shallow water potential.

OCTOBER 20

MATTHEW 15:11

"It is not what people put into their mouths that makes them unclean. It is what comes out of their mouths that makes them unclean."

HAVE YOU EVER FOUND SHAD, bluegill, or crawdad in your livewells? Not a pretty sight! Those are baitfish that bass have spit up. You can see how different they are from what they were just a short while earlier. They have gone from being something beautiful to something really ugly.

TIP

Small bodies of water can produce really big fish.

We spit up a lot of bad stuff in our lives too. Things like gossip, backbiting, lying, and malice. God knows that the bad things that come out our mouth can really cause us trouble. When we get mad or jealous or envious, we are apt to say things we don't really mean and for which we will later be ashamed. The most gracious people I know always seem to pause before they speak. Maybe they are thinking about what they say before they say it instead of after it is already said.

October 21

PROVERBS 21:21

Whoever tries to live right and be loyal
finds life, success, and honor.

When we started with ESPN about twenty-five years ago, my main concern was simply staying on the network. ESPN was not really that big back then, and I just didn't know much about the people there. They were from the North; I'm from the South, so I just hoped we could get along. Our relationship has been great and longstanding. I believe the key is that ESPN is very loyal to their show producers, and I also have been very loyal to them. We have worked together to do things correctly, and it has been good for us both.

TIP

Bass tend to scatter when water levels rise.

God sees loyalty as extremely important. It starts with loyalty to Him and being loyal to our spouse, our kids, our church, our employer, our friends. It might seem better to cut and run sometimes, but it is not God's way.

October 22

MATTHEW 25:13

"So always be ready, because you don't know the day or the hour the Son of Man will come."

I BELIEVE MY FIRST MERIT BADGE as a Boy Scout was for fishing. In fact, I qualified for that badge several times over. What really digs my memory from scouting was the Scout motto—"Be Prepared." Just think about how many fewer mistakes we would make if we daily followed that motto. We would certainly have less credit card debt, be healthier, and have more money set aside for retirement or those rainy days.

Jesus Christ is coming back. Are we ready? Is our relationship with Him strong enough today if He appears tomorrow? The world was not ready for Jesus when He first came some two thousand years ago. I don't think it's ready now either. As Christians, we must be ready, and we can be—one Christian at a time.

TIP

Hot lead weights heated by the sun can damage your fishing line.

October 23

JAMES 3:13

Are there those among you who are truly wise and understanding? Then they should show it by living right and doing good things with a gentleness that comes from wisdom.

As bass get bigger and older, they do indeed get wiser and more difficult to catch. One of their tricks is to feed mainly at night. Another is to spend most of their time about ten feet deep, a depth that a lot of fishermen don't fish.

TIP

Swim a jig around boats in floating docks, even in deep water.

In life, we are supposed to get more wisdom and understanding. What we do with these gifts is up to us. God says we show these gifts by the way we live. We do good for those around us, and we must indeed mellow with age. I am a hard-charging guy, but I do want wisdom. I want understanding. If God grants these requests, I must realize that along with wisdom and understanding come some pretty big responsibilities, especially in living right.

October 24

ISAIAH 12:2

God is the one who saves me;
I will trust him and not be afraid.

As HOOK MANUFACTURERS have developed sharper and sharper hooks, I have begun to use smaller hooks. In my worm fishing, I have moved down more than one hook size. I am now routinely using 1/0 and 2/0 hooks, where I once used 4/0 hooks. I have learned to trust those smaller, sharper hooks. I learned that trust by trying them out and catching lots of bass on small hooks. Obviously, the smaller hooks give the worms better action and produce more strikes.

TIP
Learn how deep your lure will run with different line sizes.

We learn to trust God by trying Him out as we live through situations that are hopeless without His help. It is difficult for most of us to really trust God until we have seen Him in action. Like catching a lot of bass, I have seen God work in my life a lot of times.

October 25

ACTS 17:31

God has set a day that he will judge all the world with fairness, by the man he chose long ago.

To folks not dialed into tournament fishing, some of their first questions always involve fairness. They know fishermen lie. How do we keep these guys and gals from cheating? Harold Sharp, the wise tournament director for BASS, always said the judge is in the other end of the boat. Tournament anglers are actually policed by the competitors in their boat. We are, in fact, required to report any rules violations.

TIP
Choose a lure color that matches the background.

God is watching tournaments and everything else we are doing. He sees it all, and Jesus will judge both the world and each of us. On that day, only saints will ask for justice; the rest will plead for mercy.

October 26

1 TIMOTHY 6:17

Command those who are rich with things of this world not to be proud.

FISHING IS A GAME that doesn't care who or what you are. To the fish, a person of privilege in a $40,000 Ranger Boat is pretty much the same as a barefoot ten-year-old fishing off the bank.

We will not get to heaven because of our wealth or poverty. God freely gives His grace to all. However, He does expect more out of those of us to whom He has given more. He expects us to use the things of this world for the benefit of others. This includes tithing and much more. It includes using your talents, your property, your vehicles, your money, whatever God has given you. Our biggest trap is trusting in what God has given us rather than trusting in God. This trap will always lead us into great danger.

TIP

Shad will move to the very tail end of creeks in the fall.

October 27

JOHN 20:29

Jesus told him, "You believe because you see me. Those who believe without seeing me will be truly blessed."

One of the most natural pieces of cover that fishermen sometimes pass by is a tree that has fallen into the lake on a really steep bank. The tops of such trees may be lying in water as deep as fifteen or twenty feet or more. This environment actually provides both deep and shallow cover for the fish, plus everything in between. I slow roll a Booyah Vibra-FLX spinnerbait or drop swim a jig all the way from the bank to the treetop. Often this takes a really long cast. We cannot see the top ends of the trees, but we know they are there. It's obvious.

TIP

An outgoing tide usually produces clearer and better fishing water.

Many people who looked Jesus in the eye and heard Him speak didn't believe Him. They missed the obvious. What a mystery that is, and how glorious it will be when you and I come face to face with the one who saved us.

MATTHEW 26:64

"In the future you will see the Son of Man sitting at the right hand of God."

I WON'T ARGUE about whether fall fishing is better than spring fishing, but it is pretty hard to beat a dead calm October morning with that touch of coolness in the air. That's my Rebel Pop-R time. With steam coming off the water, let that bait lie still until every ripple disappears. Don't twitch that rod tip much; just a small plop-plop is all you need. A little spit from the nose of that bait and—BANG—game on. If that is not pretty close to heaven, I'll eat your Pop-R!

TIP

Try fast-moving lures in clear water.

One day, many of us will stroll into heaven and we will see Jesus, the One who died for us. Tragically, some people will not be there. God has invited everyone. If you have not accepted Jesus as your Savior, don't wait another day.

October 29

PROVERBS 24:12

He is watching you, and he will know.
He will reward each person for what he has done.

Most of a fish's life is centered around only two things: eating and not being eaten. For a short period of time each year, they are concerned about spawning or raising babies, but then it is back to focusing on getting food and not becoming food. Everything else is secondary.

TIP
Fish a spinnerbait at a depth just before you lose sight of it.

Because we know God is always watching and all-knowing, what should our lives be centered on? For some of us, our focus is the same as the fish—food—but our lives should revolve around God and what He wants for us. Godly living, godly loving, godly caring, godly sharing, godly attitudes. The Bible says God has a reward for each of us, and I am pretty sure it is not shad for dinner.

October 30

1 PETER 4:14

When people insult you because you follow Christ, you are blessed.

THE BEER PATCH situation has been widely publicized in both Christian and non-Christian circles. Most stories center around the points I lost, the money passed up, the chastisement I received, or how I was hurt or penalized by not wearing that patch or placing the beer decal on my boat. What has been missed are all the blessings my God has showered down because of it. The publicity has given me even more opportunities to share the gospel than ever before. We have been in more churches and talked to more non-Christian sportsmen than ever before. There are men in heaven right now who made that important decision to accept Jesus during one of these events. When we suffer, God has all the ability in the world to turn that into great victory.

TIP

Always try to make your first cast to a target perfect.

October 31

ROMANS 8:14

The true children of God are those who let God's Spirit lead them.

MOST OF US learned to fish from Mom and Dad. Fishing is a family sport, and most parents who fish get a lot of pleasure teaching their children about it. We also have a tendency to like the same lures and types of techniques that our parents like. If Dad likes buzzbaits, we like buzzbaits. Dad has instilled that in us.

That is what God wants from you and me. He wants us to act and react just as He would to everyday happenings in our lives. How would God react if He were fired, sued, cheated, lied to, divorced, left out, or bad-mouthed? How does He want us to react? By praying in the Spirit that God has placed in all of us who are saved.

TIP

Bass are lazy, so make it easy for them to "eat" your lure.

November

NOVEMBER 1

PHILIPPIANS 2:14

Do everything without complaining or arguing.

MY GRANDCHILDREN—Jeremy, Kyle, Jordyn, and even the younger ones, Kutler and Merrick—have all been exposed to great fishing experiences. They have fished out of the very best boats made. They have had the very best rods and reels in their hands with the best lures tied on the ends of the very best lines. Of course, they get to fish in water teeming with fish, yet they start complaining pretty quickly if they don't get a bite. The younger ones are the worst. They complain even more if someone else is catching fish and they aren't. Childish? Sure, but don't we carry this childish behavior into our adult lives? You bet we do. And that is not at all what God wants. When you catch yourself starting to complain about something today, talk about a blessing or two instead.

TIP

Pick your bait for the spot and type of cover you are fishing.

November 2

ISAIAH 49:16

See, I have written your name on my hand.

At our Keys High School football game one week, my granddaughter, Jordyn, got into one of her "Granddad's autograph" modes. She was having me sign programs, paper cups, and anything else she could find. Of course she had all of her little friends doing the same. When they ran out of things, they proudly presented their hands. I obliged by signing with a permanent marker and now have several moms mad at me, including my daughter-in-law.

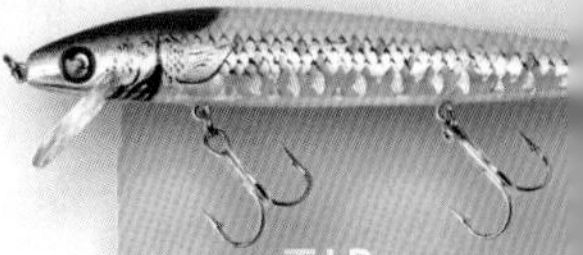

TIP

Larger line works better on a Pop-R or a Zara Spook.

Think about having your name written on the Hand that formed you, the Hand that created the oceans. You can't get any more special than that. Just think, God looks down and sees your name right there every day.

November 3

HEBREWS 13:20

I pray that the God of peace will give you every good thing you need so you can do what he wants.

When you hear pros talk about making a milk run in tournaments, what do they mean? Making a milk run is laying out a tournament day where you systematically stop and fish several different spots. Each spot must have something that you believe will allow you to catch at least one fish there.

TIP

You can pretty much stick to a jig in cold, muddy water.

God has promised to give us exactly what we need to excel in this milk run of life so that we can do His will. Whatever talents, whatever skills, whatever money or time we have are direct gifts from God. He also has given us the choice to use all these gifts for our glory or for His. How can you use your good things today to do what God wants?

PROVERBS 3:30

Don't accuse someone who has not harmed you.

ON A REALLY LARGE LAKE, one of the easiest ways to locate bass is to find a major creek that has everything a bass needs. That creek becomes the entire lake for the fish because they never leave, no matter the conditions or the time of year. They feel safe, have places to spawn, and have plenty of food.

A sin that has everything it needs to dwell in our spirits and haunt us is, saying something bad about others. Most of the time, we've spouted off about a situation that has not hurt us and, often, one we are not involved in at all. I have been on the receiving end of accusations coming from folks I didn't even know and who were not involved. The hurt and pain are very real. Let us hold our tongues (and our e-mails) and remember that making false accusations is a sin that causes others unnecessary pain.

TIP

Small holes in matted cover should be fished with a pegged slip sinker.

November 5

JAMES 5:13

Anyone who is having troubles should pray.

CASTING ANGLES can be just as important as locating fish. Most of the time, we are around some fish, but catching them can be tricky. I think it is really important for a fisherman to stand up when bass fishing. This will dramatically improve your angles to your target, especially if you are flippin', pitchin', or makin' short casts.

TIP

Bass actually hear (feel vibrations) with their lateral line.

It is really important for a Christian to pray in order to flourish in life. God knows what we are going through. He knows all the angles of every situation. We are not praying to let God know what troubles we have; rather, we are praying to include God in the problem-solving. God wants to be the solution, not just a part of it. A great deal of the time, I find I have a problem because I left God out in the first place.

November 6

PHILIPPIANS 2:5

In your lives you must think and act like Christ Jesus.

DID YOU EVER WISH you could think like Roland Martin, Larry Nixon, Bill Dance, Kevin VanDam, or Hank Parker? What if you had the fishing knowledge of all these men stored inside your head? Then all you would need to catch fish would be the water.

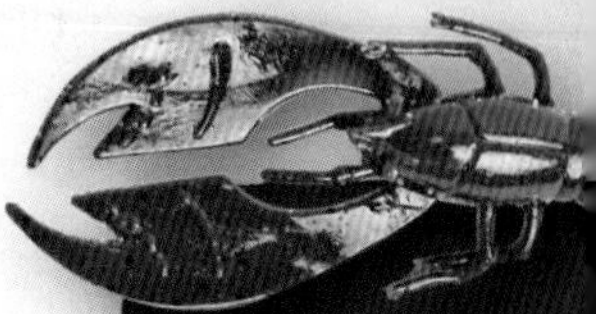

TIP

Choose a crankbait that will run deep enough to hit some structure or cover.

How about thinking and acting like Jesus Himself? That opportunity is available, and it is far better than having the know-how of all the superstar fishermen put together. Jesus experienced everything you and I will ever face. He struggled against the same adversary, the devil, and He conquered. He died, just as we will, and His resurrection proved we can and will live again also. Jesus has given us His very Spirit so that we can be like Him.

November 7

1 JOHN 4:4

God's Spirit, who is in you, is greater than the devil, who is in the world.

Occasionally someone gets into my boat who is particularly foul-mouthed. This is a little rare, but when it happens, those words really stand out. Usually that person will apologize, but will continue to slip from time to time throughout the day. It is a pretty safe bet that God's Spirit does not live in that person.

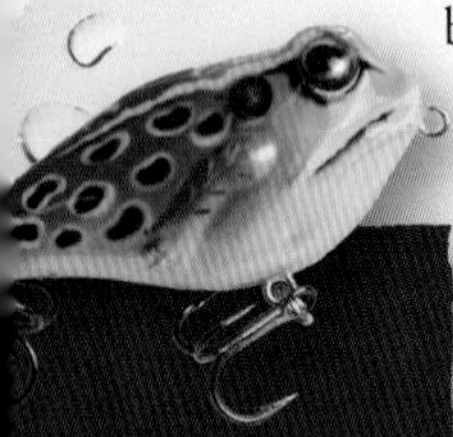

TIP

Standing up while fishing will allow you to see more underwater cover.

But even if God's Spirit is present, I believe the devil is constantly trying to push God out and claim a little territory for himself. I know I let the devil win some ground at times. The problem is that if we let the devil get his foot in the door, he will try to kick the door down and take over our whole house. Thankfully, we have a weapon. That weapon is God's Spirit, and if we use it, Satan will go running every time.

2 THESSALONIANS 2:13

Brothers and sisters, whom the Lord loves, God chose you from the beginning to be saved.

IT IS FUN TO WATCH the nonboaters at our pre-tournament pairings. Most have paid their entry money in hopes of drawing Denny Brauer, Roland Martin, or another of the big name superstars. You can see people's elation when they do and also their disappointment when they get someone they have never heard of.

TIP

If it is important to the fish, make it important to you.

We should be overjoyed to learn that God has chosen us to go fishing with Him. We should also be very thankful. So thankful that we work extra hard to be obedient to Him. In order to please God, we must work extra hard to love one another and forgive one another. No matter how tough life gets, no matter how big our problems, just think—God chose us. That fact is not only bigger, it is better than anything this world has to offer.

November 9

1 PETER 5:4

Then when Christ, the Chief Shepherd, comes, you will get a glorious crown that will never lose its beauty.

WHEN I FIRST SAW a Terminator spinnerbait, it was—and still is—the prettiest spinnerbait I have ever seen. The gold-plated blade was shinier than any other on the market. The fish-like metalized head was awesome and looked so real. The quick-change skirt with two sizes of rubber tails had incredible action. It was really more a work of art than a fishing lure. The frame was made of spaceage titanium. I was, to say the least, very impressed.

TIP

You can tell if the tide is going in or out by looking at weeds or anchored boats.

As pretty as that Terminator looked, it will not come close to what God has in store for you and me. Not a halo, but a crown more glorious and more beautiful than we can ever imagine. And, unlike the spinnerbait that gets pretty ragged after forty or fifty bass, our crown will look just as amazing after a thousand years.

JAMES 3:16

Where jealousy and selfishness are, there will be confusion and every kind of evil.

ONE OF THE WAYS to fish a large flat is to drift and simply drag your lure behind the boat. This works well with a Carolina Rig or a tube. On lakes like Sam Rayburn in Texas, we have flats with irregular bottoms. Drifting works great in these areas. I always keep a marker buoy handy and pitch it overboard when I get a strike.

TIP

Most bass in rivers can be caught less than four or five feet deep.

Although we are saved, most of us have a tendency to drag sins along with us for a long time. One sin that is hard to leave behind is jealousy. It is hard, many times, to feel good about someone else's success, particularly if it is someone you compete with. God says jealousy produces evil. He equates jealousy with evil. Most of us don't look at ourselves as evil, but what does God see?

November 11

GALATIANS 3:28

In Christ, there is no difference between Jew and Greek, slave and free person, male and female. You are all the same in Christ Jesus.

AT A SPORTSMAN'S JAMBOREE recently in Columbia, South Carolina, I had the chance to tour the historic First Baptist Church where the event was held. The gorgeous new sanctuary holds over three thousand people. What intrigued me, though, was the original sanctuary where the pastor, Wendell Estep, explained the seating. The lower area was for the free men; the upper seating, a surrounding balcony, was for the slaves. The platform where the preaching was done was at a height an equal distance between the two seating areas. This signified that even though men separated themselves, God sees no difference. Praise God, His impartiality is exactly what allows you and me to be saved.

TIP
Make your casts upstream when fishing in a current.

November 12

1 CORINTHIANS 13:7

Love patiently accepts all things. It always trusts, always hopes, and always endures.

FISHING IS A PARTICIPATION SPORT. Over sixty million Americans fish. Some of these sixty million like to fish, but most *love* to fish. Those of us who love fishing patiently endure whatever the sport throws at us—bad weather, bad lakes, bad partners, and even the dreaded lockjaw when the fish refuse to bite—we still love, we still hope.

God has commanded us to love one another no matter what. He did not recommend we love or suggest we love—He *commanded* it. With this godly love comes a huge commitment to one another, and this commitment includes forgiveness. If you harbor anything in your mind that requires forgiveness, do it right now. For love to remain strong, it must accept all things, including wrong, and forgive.

TIP

Use desiccant packets in your tackle box to help eliminate moisture and prevent rusty hooks.

GENESIS 4:7

If you do things well, I will accept you, but if you do not do them well, sin is ready to attack you. Sin wants you, but you must rule over it.

THE ELEMENTS play a big part of any day's fishing. (Most of the perfect days occur when we have to work and can't go fishing!) Wind, rain, hot, cold, high water, low water, muddy, clear—every situation can pose a problem. The better fisherman you become, the more you will be able to use different circumstances to your benefit.

TIP

Wind direction will predictably position bass on structure or cover.

God expects us to excel. He wants us to succeed and do things well in every circumstance. He will not abandon us when we don't do as well as we should, but He does give a warning. When we goof off, sin will be there to pounce on us. We either rule over sin with God's help, or sin will rule over us. Make a commitment to excel in your life's circumstances, and you will reap His rewards.

HEBREWS 13:5

Keep your lives free from the love of money,
and be satisfied with what you have.

CLEAR WATER is a lot of fun to fish, but it can be pretty frustrating if we are not willing to change our tactics a bit. The simplest way is to move to light line, four- to eight-pound test, and small lures. My choices are one-eighth-ounce spinnerbaits, tiny crankbaits, Blakemore Road Runners, and four-inch finesse worms. These small lures will attract fish and lots of strikes, but you will need to be satisfied with smaller bass.

TIP

Use a shad-colored spinnerbait when fall water temps drop to the low- to mid-sixties.

Most of us have a hard time being satisfied with less. It's hard not to want or pursue money. We work harder and longer hours. We change jobs. How do we balance our needs and our family's needs, yet still please and obey God? We must be satisfied with what God gives each of us, because the most important part of life is not money. It's Jesus.

November 15

HEBREWS 12:25

So be careful and do not refuse to listen when God speaks.

I HAVE ALWAYS believed we would one day have an underwater speaker, perhaps attached to our trolling motor, that would transmit sounds under the water to help trigger strikes. Maybe we could talk to the fish, using the sound of active shad or schooling bass. I am actually using such a unit right now called Biosonix, and I have had some pretty positive results.

TIP

Catch shad below dams for great catfish bait.

Is God talking to His people today? Yes! Does He talk to us individually? Again, yes. During my most trying and difficult situations, my God has always been there. He talks to me as I pray, listen to sermons, read His Word, or worship Him with music. He has given me answers, reasons, and comfort. I could not make it without Him. Trust me, God will speak. Just listen.

1 PETER 3:13

If you are trying hard to do good,
no one can really hurt you.

IF YOU SPEND much time with fishermen, pro or amateur, you will soon hear stories of bad days turning into huge victories. You find this true in just about any profession. Most everyone fails a lot before succeeding. Keep on trying hard and never give up. In fishing tournaments, judges never keep score of all the casts that didn't get a strike. They only put on the scales the ones that did.

TIP
Your first cast in a brush pile should be on the edge.

Jesus wants us working hard at doing good, no matter what results we are getting. He even says we cannot really be harmed as long as we are working hard to benefit others. We wonder why bad things happen to us when we are working so hard to do God's work. Don't get frustrated; don't give up. Jesus has your victory just around the corner.

NOVEMBER 17

ROMANS 11:5

There are a few people that God has chosen by his grace.

IN NOVEMBER 2004, America chose its president. They chose one of my fishing friends, George W. Bush. Long before America re-elected George W. Bush; long before his dad was president; even long before I first met George W. in Pine Bluff, Arkansas, when his father was the vice president, God chose George W. Bush. He chose him for something much greater being than president of the United States. God chose him to be saved from hell to be with Him in heaven.

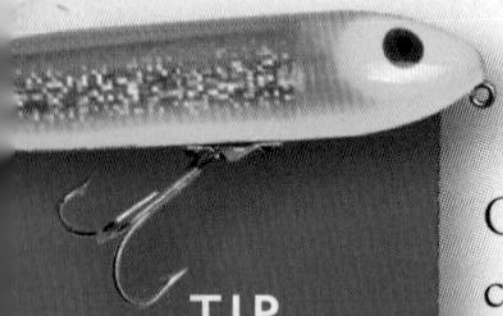

TIP

Willow leaf blades allow your spinnerbait to get deeper quicker.

Chosen by God's grace. We need only to accept that grace, so freely given. President George W. Bush accepted that grace. I have accepted it. Have you?

November 18

MARK 4:24

"The way you give to others is the way God will give to you, but God will give you even more."

We spend so much time with our grandchildren fishing, hunting, birthday parties, ballgames, and just being with them. We often revolve our entire schedule around them. No matter how much time, how much attention, how much love we give, we seem to always get back more.

God says it will be that way with Him. We cannot outgive God. Many believing Christians have tested this, and I have yet to hear it not be true. Help others, and see how much God helps you. Increase your tithes and offerings, and see what God does. God is a rewarding God. He has our greatest reward ready and waiting—heaven! He also has plenty of rewards to give us right here on earth.

TIP

You can turn a floating jerkbait into a suspending jerkbait by simply adding Storm SuspenStrips.

November 19

DEUTERONOMY 4:34

He did it with tests, signs, miracles, war, and great sights, by his great power and strength.

THERE ARE MAYBE millions of unfished bass in the United States. We have more small pieces of water available that have never had a bass lure tossed into them than you can shake your favorite spinnerbait rod at. Most of the water holes are around cities and towns. They are around shopping centers, golf courses, housing developments, abandoned gravel pits, and other unsuspecting spots.

We might overlook some super fishing holes, but we cannot possibly overlook the awesome power of an almighty God. God displays His great power every day. Even a nonbeliever outdoorsman sees this. To those of us who are believers, we not only see these miracles and great sights every day, but we have come to cherish them.

TIP

Add a split shot to small spinnerbaits for easier casting.

TITUS 2:8

Speak the truth so that you cannot be criticized.

WHEN THE WATER TEMPERATURE starts dropping in the winter, the temperature you want to really watch for is 58 degrees. When the water hits that magic number, bass will generally be most active. This is probably the best spinnerbait temperature you will see until springtime. Once the water temperature falls a few degrees below 58, bass fishing will become more difficult.

TIP

Try to not let your shadow fall onto a target you are fishing.

Complete truthfulness is a "magical" quality to develop in your personal and professional life. In today's world, it is a rarity. Personally, I know only a few people I can count on to tell me the truth under all circumstances. When you are tempted to bend the truth a little or just flat outright lie—don't.

NOVEMBER 21

LEVITICUS 18:26

You must obey my laws and rules, and you must not do any of those hateful sins.

LIKE POINTS ARE TO A LAKE, wing dams are to a river. If you know nothing else about a lake, you can go from point to point and have a good chance of catching fish. Do the same with wing dams. They always hold bait, have rock and wood cover, and direct the way the current flows. The breaks and cut-out areas will almost always produce eddies where fish will wait for something to eat.

TIP

Use the cold winter months to clean and organize all your tackle to get ready for that great spring fishin'.

God's laws should direct the currents of our lives. As long as we live according to how He tells us to live, we will have few problems. Break these rules, and we must suffer the consequences. God doesn't want to see us hurt or suffer. He wants to see us content and full of joy. The happiest you and I will ever be is when we are faithfully obeying God.

November 22

JAMES 5:16

When a believing person prays, great things happen.

When the water cools into the fifties or lower and the bass become less active, you've got to both slow down and change lures. I like the new Yumbrella Swimbait Rig, the Bomber 9A Crankbait, and a 3/4- to 1-ounce Booyah Spinnerbait. Fish deeper and you'll get more strikes and hook huge bass, especially in clear water.

When difficulties arise in our lives and the lives of people we know, prayer is the key. God is always in the active mode of answering prayer. Every believer can testify to answered prayer. I have friends alive today because of answered prayer. Never—and I mean *never*—underestimate what God has the power to do. Never stop praying.

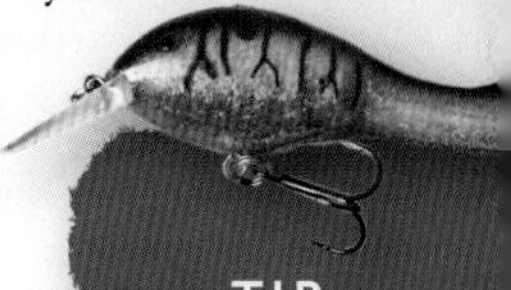

TIP

Nose hook a finesse worm on a drop shot rig on smooth bottoms in ultraclear water.

November 23

1 PETER 2:9

You were chosen to tell about the wonderful acts of God, who called you out of darkness into his wonderful light.

Bass feed at night and are easier to catch then. Really dark nights, though, are all but impossible without some help. Lights of some kind—from boat docks, black lights, or even the moon finally peeking over the mountains—are both welcome and extremely necessary.

TIP
Learn the "fishing-line" trick for easy hook removal from just about any part of the human body.

Without God, it's like our very being is groping around on a pitchblack lake. Jesus is the light that brightens our lives. He lights us up so we can lead others to Him. If you are saved, God is doing some great things in your life right now. Share that with someone today and watch God brighten up his or her world.

November 24

GENESIS 15:6

Abram believed the Lord. And the Lord accepted Abram's faith, and that faith made him right with God.

Awhile back, I fished with an eleven-year-old named Austin in Alabama. He knew so much about fishing and hunting that it was like fishing with a small adult. He had learned most of this knowledge from his granddad. I love to fish with kids because they hang on every little bit of instruction and believe what you are teaching them is absolutely true.

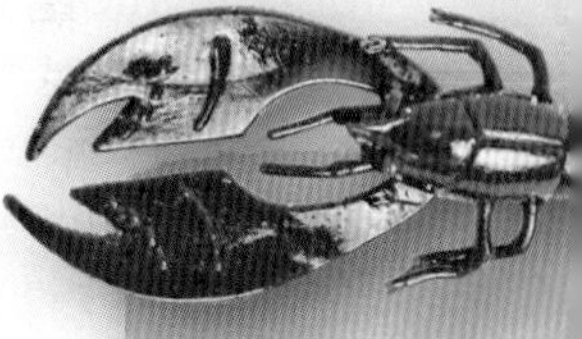

TIP
Learn to make short, accurate casts.

We are all little children to God, and what He has to teach us is 100 percent true. All God asks is that we believe. We are to believe with all we have and know that God is able to accomplish everything He has promised. It is this faith that makes us right with God. What a great Father we have in this God we serve.

November 25

MATTHEW 5:16

"You should be a light for other people. Live so that they will see the good things you do and will praise your Father in heaven."

TOURNAMENT FISHERMEN live for recognition in magazine articles, television, radio, newspapers, Internet . . . anything to get their names out there. Some have big egos, but most just need the recognition to promote their current sponsors and attract new ones.

TIP

Fish depend more on smell and sound in muddy water.

As Christians, we should be walking, talking billboards for Jesus. Everything we do and say should shine a bright, positive light on our Savior, Jesus Christ. Oftentimes, my light shines pretty dim. But when we think of what Jesus did for us, how He helps us every day, and what He has prepared for us, how can we justify doing anything less than shine brightly? Let's make today a day that glorifies Jesus by the way we live it.

NOVEMBER 26

PSALM 42:1

As a deer thirsts for streams of water,
so I thirst for you, God.

THE BIGGEST DEER I have ever taken with a bow in Oklahoma came when I was just a teenager. It was a twelve-point with massive horns and long tines. I shot the buck about forty-five minutes before dark. I had been in the tree since before daylight. The key to success that day? It was an extremely dry year, and I was hunting a small pond, the only water in the entire area. Every deer for miles around had to come to that water.

TIP

Try shortening your plastic worms under tough conditions, even down to three or four inches.

Jesus called Himself the living water. He is, in fact, the only living water available for you and me. For eternal life, we must come to Jesus. He is our only option.

November 27

PROVERBS 10:12

Hatred stirs up trouble,
but love forgives all wrong.

My wife, Chris, is a great fishing partner and a great partner in life, and whatever challenges come against us, we face them together. Not everyone is so blessed. Having a partner who constantly focuses on faults can produce discord and turmoil—to the point of killing the relationship. So it's vital to overlook someone's shortcomings and focus on the good. True love is indeed blind.

God made love so strong, so powerful, that it absolutely has the power to forgive the most grievous of wrongs we do to one another. This is a gift from God, and it is exactly how God loves us. His love is so great, so binding, so eternal, that no matter how bad we are, He forgives. He has provided Jesus to make our marriage to Him complete. He's the Partner we all can always count on.

TIP

A GPS unit on the bow of your boat will give you an extra advantage.

1 CORINTHIANS 13:13

So these three things continue forever: faith, hope, and love. And the greatest of these is love.

WHEN YOU HAVE BEEN FISHING and living with the same woman for over forty-five years, you learn a great deal about love and just how powerful God really made it. As I look back and realize just how much I love Chris today, I wonder if I was really in love at all forty-five years ago. I am sure I was, but love is like a rubber plant that grows beyond our wildest imagination. I could never imagine loving a woman this much, and I miss her almost immediately when we are apart. As great and strong as that love is, I believe God's love for her and for me is even greater. God's love was carried all the way to the Cross some two thousand years ago, and I believe God's love has grown every day since.

TIP

A snap attached to the split ring will give a jerkbait a wider wobble.

NOVEMBER 29

1 CORINTHIANS 3:9

We are God's workers, working together; you are like God's farm, God's house.

I HAVE ALMOST as much fun managing my fishing lake as I do actually catching fish. I spend a lot of time making the fishing better and the fish bigger and more productive. We fertilize; we feed; we build spawning areas; we haul shad; we add cover; we do whatever it takes to improve all aspects of our lake.

TIP

Fish into the sun whenever possible to avoid casting a shadow.

Shouldn't we get just as excited about working for the God who has done so much for us? Together we can feed, love, teach, forgive, lift up, encourage, and improve everyone around us. We can and should make a difference for God every single day of our lives. The most amazing thing is that when we make a difference for God, He makes an even bigger difference in us.

November 30

1 PETER 1:7

These troubles come to prove that your faith is pure.

BASS FISHING, especially tournament fishing, is definitely a moving target. In order to really stay at the top of the game, you must fish every situation as it comes to you. We must actually fish the day, the hour, the moment, and even each cast according to a wide range of variables. To figure out these variables, we rely on our skills, abilities, and experiences.

TIP

You can add glitter to a blade or crankbait with clear fingernail polish.

Troubles, like changes in fishing, come along regularly. They come as a check on our faith. Is our faith strong enough to rely on God, or do we run from God? I have learned that I must rely on God. The bigger the problem, the more I need God. After all these years my God has never failed me. Not even once.

December

December 1

JOHN 11:44

The dead man came out, his hands and feet wrapped with pieces of cloth, and a cloth around his face.

MOST PEOPLE who fish from boats have long since given up carrying fish stringers. Some younger bass anglers probably don't even know what a stringer is. We now use sophisticated livewells and chemicals to keep our fish alive.

Today's verse is about the famous Lazarus. After Lazarus had been dead for four days and was smelling bad, Jesus raised him with just three words, "Lazarus, come out!" This is the business Jesus is all about—renewing life—but before He raises us from physical death, we must admit our death and ask forgiveness to receive this spiritual life. Jesus is the Life-Giver, and if you haven't yet received that life, choose to do so today.

TIP

You can change the depth of a crankbait by simply raising or lowering your rod tip.

December 2

JOB 33:12

God is greater than we are.

IT IS PRETTY EASY to listen and pay attention if Jay Yelas or Roland Martin starts talking about how to catch bass. Most people believe these pros know more about catching bass than they themselves do. Listening to their buddies in their bass clubs is a different story. What causes this? Pride, unbelief, the feeling you know more than the other guy does? But what if he really can help you?

TIP

Don't be afraid to try new lures, techniques, or ideas.

How often do we do think we know more than God in our daily struggles? The last time I checked, God is still God and I'm not. He is also more powerful than the most awesome thing or event we could ever imagine. Do we really think we could do a better job without Him? Try God today. Include Him in every aspect of your life today and then survey the results tonight.

December 3

HEBREWS 12:1

So let us run the race that is before us and never give up.

YOU WILL NEVER HEAR a champion fisherman say he knew he was beaten after the first few hours of competition. Always believing and never stopping are the keys to success in whatever we are doing.

TIP

When fishing gets tough, try slipping a piece of Alka-Seltzer inside a tube bait.

Life is certain to throw many roadblocks in front of us. Troubles will come, but God is always able to overcome. We just need to hang in there and do our best with whatever God has equipped us. God will always reward our efforts. Will we always succeed, always win? In the short haul, victory is a moving target. But in the long haul, for eternity, Jesus has provided for those who believe in Him the certainty of absolute victory. Let's never give up.

DECEMBER 4

PROVERBS 5:21

The Lord *sees everything you do,*
and he watches where you go.

I KNOW OF VERY FEW FISHERMEN who have not cast a lure into water where they were not supposed to fish. Most hunters have ventured onto land—at least for a few feet—that they were not allowed on. Would this have happened if the owner or a game warden were looking on? I don't think so.

Why in the world do we say things, go places, and do things as if God can't see or hear or know what we're up to? Surprise! He knows, hears, and sees everything. We actually should live our lives in constant awareness that we mess up, and praise God that, in His huge grace, He completely forgives every wrong that He has ever seen us do.

TIP

Larger blades will give a spinnerbait more lift.

December 5

1 CORINTHIANS 2:5

[My preaching did not offer human wisdom] so that your faith would be in God's power and not in human wisdom.

WE SPEND OUR ENTIRE LIVES trying to get smarter about fishing. It is a fact: the more we know about the fish, the water, the weather, and the time of the year, the more likely we will have success. We rely mostly on our own smarts, but often we need help.

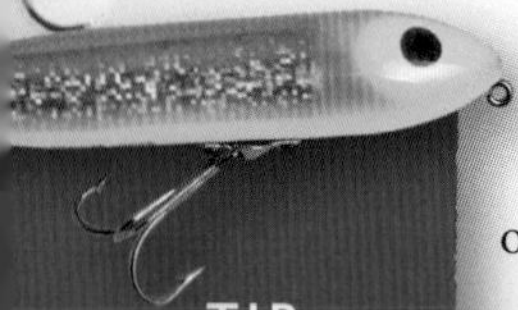

TIP

The calmer the water, the farther a bass will usually travel to get your topwater lure.

Trying to solve our problems just by being smart is foolish. The fact is, God generally will let us get deeper and deeper into trouble until we call on Him for help. God requires that we completely trust in Him. He allows us to get into dire situations in order to grow our faith. If all went well every day, we wouldn't need to put our faith in much of anything. Problems grow faith.

December 6

1 JOHN 3:18

We should love people not only with words and talk, but by our actions and true caring.

Everyone I run into has a fishing story. Some are true, but many are not. I have heard most of the fishing jokes several times. I still listen, and I still enjoy the stories and the funnies. I listen because I care for the people telling the stories.

We all like to talk—me more than most. The problem is that most of today's society is not listening. People are not listening because their hearts and minds are so centered upon themselves. They really care about no one else.

TIP

In the wintertime, the afternoon bite is usually better.

If we want to be more like Jesus Christ today, we simply must listen. This works at home, at work, at church, virtually everywhere. It is so powerful that it will even work with a total stranger. Listen to someone today.

December 7

ISAIAH 59:1

Surely the LORD's power is enough to save you.
He can hear you when you ask him for help.

WE TRUST COMPLETELY in God's ability to take us to heaven, to save us from hell and to give us eternal life with Him. But how much does He care about our problems with our boss, our money, our friends? Is God really concerned when we have a spat with our spouse or get wronged in a business deal? You bet He is!

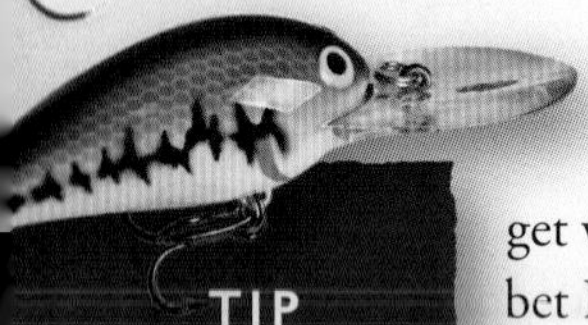

TIP

On topwater lures, you can coat the last foot or so of line with fly line dressing.

God tells us that if we can be trusted with just a little, He will trust us with a lot. We can certainly trust Him with everything, no matter how big or how small. Whatever our needs, God will always listen. When no one else seems to care, God does. When we are frustrated, God will encourage. No one cares more about us than the God who made us.

DECEMBER 8

MATTHEW 19:23

"It will be hard for a rich person to enter the kingdom of heaven."

LUKE CLAUSON received $500,000 by winning the 2004 FLW Championship. At the tender age of twenty-five, Luke had won in four days more than many pros had won in a lifetime.

Riches, of course, must be measured in more than money. How can riches keep us away from God and make it nearly impossible to get to heaven? Because wealth so often rearranges our priorities. God's desire is to be the only Lord of our life. He will not play second fiddle to anything, especially money. When we put God first, He will provide the riches we need. Even wealth, though it can be a trap. So when God blesses you with riches, be very careful to keep them in their proper place—below, not above, God.

TIP

Try a floating worm on a weighted hook in deep clear water.

DECEMBER 9

LUKE 10:18

"I saw Satan fall like lightning from heaven."

RECENTLY, PAT TURNER and I spent three days in Kentucky bow hunting. We experienced some of the most spectacular and severe lightning I have ever seen. Pat was in one tree with a metal camera and a metal camera brace. I was a few feet away in another tree with my metal PSE bow and carbon arrow. We were twenty-four feet high, sitting on metal, lock-on Summit tree stands. I watched lightning strike faster than a heartbeat.

TIP

A wacky rigged worm will work even in the wintertime.

If God hurled the rebellious devil from heaven that quickly, how can He stand to look on the rebellion and sin we daily commit? He can't, but He doesn't need to see our sin because of what Jesus has done for you and me. Jesus died to remove our sins from His Father, almighty God.

December 10

HEBREWS 12:2

Let us look only to Jesus, the One who began our faith and who makes it perfect.

I HAVE SAID MANY TIMES that the only perfect cast is one that comes back with a fish attached to the end of it. Perfect casts are hard to come by, and some days they hardly happen at all.

Jesus is the sole, perfect reason for our faith. Without Jesus, we would have no hope of forgiveness, no hope for grace or mercy, no chance for eternity, and no real reason for living.

Jesus is where our eyes must focus daily. Jesus is where we look to handle life's problems, both big and small. Jesus is a Friend when we are lonely; a Safety Net when we are scared. Jesus loves, He heals, He strengthens, He encourages. Is there really anything or anyone else in whom we could have perfect faith?

TIP

Build brush piles in cold weather when the sap has drained to the bottom of the trees.

DECEMBER 11

1 JOHN 1:9

If we confess our sins, he will forgive our sins, because we can trust God to do what is right.

AT LAKE OKEECHOBEE a few years back, Chris and I were catching a few bass out of pepper grass pods on worms. We tried several colors until Chris hit upon purple with a yellow tail. This color combination outproduced any other color by a wide margin. I finished in the top ten by fishing the right pattern with the right bait in the right color.

TIP

Bass get very conditioned to current and power plant generation patterns.

We serve a God who will always do right by us. He knows the right pattern for our lives. He loves us more than we can ever know. God wants only the best for us, and when we humble ourselves and confess our sins, we become God's children. Even as God corrects us when we fail Him, we can most assuredly count on God to do the right thing for us.

2 THESSALONIANS 2:17

God loved us, and through his grace he gave us a good hope and encouragement that continues forever.

ONCE WE LEARN HOW TO CAST, we continually learn how to cast better. And the better we cast, the more fish we catch. Fishing is not something we need to relearn every time we go to the lake.

Once we are saved, we are saved forever and that, of course, goes way beyond this temporal life here on earth. This belief should be our focus every time trouble pops up in our lives. God's grace is our ticket to joy and happiness, no matter how bad things are during our greatest struggles. Instead of dwelling on what is wrong today, we should think about what our lives will be like a thousand years from now. We have a God who loves us immensely, and He proves it every single day. Our job is merely to trust Him and accept that mighty love He so freely gives!

TIP

During cold fronts, bass get into the thickest cover possible.

December 13

PSALM 100:3

Know that the Lord is God.
He made us, and we belong to him;
we are his people, the sheep he tends.

It is so enjoyable to see our kids and grandchildren grow in their fishing abilities. Over time and offering a great deal of patience, we watch them improve, learn, and then become creative in the ways they fish. They go from no knowledge at all to figuring out better ways to catch fish. What a thrill that is to watch!

TIP
Bass will load up under dead leaves in the tail end of pockets in the fall and early winter.

Our God is constantly watching and looking out for each of us. As we created our kids, He created us. He must really get excited as we grow in Christ. Our own children are so proud when they accomplish something, and they know we share in their joy. God feels the same way about you and me. Our daily goal should be to make God proud of His creation—us!

December 14

PSALM 147:5

Our Lord is great and very powerful.
There is no limit to what he knows.

FISHING AND HUNTING rules are built around limits. Limits are what we use to make these activities better. Limits for bass have decreased over the years from ten or fifteen bass down to five or six. Limits for deer and turkey have, on the other hand, increased just about everywhere.

TIP
Just a few degrees change in water temperature makes a big difference to fish.

Whether we like it or acknowledge it, God has placed limits on each of us. He did this so we can't become God. He is God; I'm not! God does have the potential to stretch our limits far beyond what we can do alone. And the great thing is that He wants to!

When you feel you have reached your limit in whatever you are trying to accomplish, ask God to move the boundaries, to stretch them out a bit. I have seen Him do it many times.

December 15

EXODUS 3:12

God said, "I will be with you."

PAY CLOSE ATTENTION to how deep you hook a fish. This can give you some really good information. If a fish is hooked deep or swallows your hook, there are probably more fish on that spot. A fish barely hooked might indicate few fish or tell you to make some changes in your lure or your presentation. How a fish is hooked will almost always tell you something.

TIP

Fish for snook in saltwater with the same lures and tactics you use for bass.

God has told us from Genesis through Revelation that He will always be with us. He has never wavered throughout time. Sure, there have been many times when I have left God, but God has always been there to welcome me back. As I have grown older and hopefully a bit wiser, I try very hard to never leave God out of anything I do. I'm hooked on Him, but even more, He's hooked on me!

December 16

HEBREWS 4:16

Let us, then, feel very sure that we can come before God's throne where there is grace.

At the Bass Pro Shop in Toronto, Canada, I visited with many folks who were planning trips to the South. They were going to Florida, Mexico, even Oklahoma to go bass fishing. By contrast, in the South in the summertime, we get excited about going north to Canada to fish.

One day we will go to the most exciting place there is—to the throne of God Himself. We can approach that throne with giant smiles, because the throne overflows with the grace that Jesus has provided to His saved flock. This promise is ours because of our faith and trust in Jesus. What a great day and terrific feeling that will be when God looks down from that throne and smiles back.

TIP

Drill holes in buzzbaits and spinnerbait blades to create bubbles.

DECEMBER 17

HEBREWS 13:2

Remember to welcome strangers, because some who have done this have welcomed angels without knowing it.

SEVERAL YEARS AGO, the Benefit 4 Kids organization contacted me about taking a little boy fishing who had been diagnosed with stage four Rhabdomyosarcoma when he was almost three years old. We were a little apprehensive about accepting the request because we didn't know if he was old enough to *really* fish. Boy, were we wrong!

Timmy's fishing ability and his desire to fish were unbelievable. We actually invited him and his parents back for a second trip just shortly before he died—just two years after being diagnosed.

TIP

Timmy liked big baits, and big–baits are sometimes the key to catching big fish.

What a blessing we would have missed if we had not had the privilege of meeting Timmy Larson. His mother called him her angel boy and I would have to agree. He was definitely our "angel" visitor.

December 18

REVELATION 21:8

Those who refuse to believe, who do evil things, who kill, who sin sexually, who do evil magic, who worship idols, and who tell lies—all these will have a place in the lake of burning sulfur.

One of the best places to fish a spinnerbait is in the heaviest possible cover you can find, the nastier the better. Get close, make short accurate casts, and bring that Booyah through that cover from several different angles. Just a slight change in angle can often produce strikes.

TIP
Always make as little noise as possible in clear or calm water.

The worst place I can think of is hell, a literal lake of fire. Why would anyone refuse to believe God and therefore have hell as their destination for eternity? Nothing in this life can be as bad as hell really is. Trusting in Jesus Christ will totally remove that destination from anyone's itinerary. If you're not saved, don't let another day go by without making Jesus your Lord.

DECEMBER 19

2 TIMOTHY 3:1–2

In the last days there will be many troubles,
because people will love themselves,
love money, brag, and be proud.

ARE WE IN THE LAST DAYS, the days just before Jesus comes back to Earth? Are things really bad enough? Well, it certainly seems so! Worldwide, colossal troubles do prevail. Individuals, leaders, and countries make their policies and decisions based on money. Throughout God's Bible, He prophesies or makes predictions, and all come true. Will we soon see Jesus riding on the clouds, arriving with a shout? Even more important, are you and I ready? I am. If you are not, I would make that your top priority. Today might just very well be *that day*.

TIP

To stripe a lure, use a comb and spray paint.

PROVERBS 31:28

Her husband also praises her.

I OFTEN BRAG that, after over forty-five years of marriage, I am an expert on marriage, perhaps even an expert on women. The truth is, I am only an expert on marriage to one specific woman, and my expertise about her is still in the learning stage.

I can tell you guys one thing, though: brag about your woman. Lift her up and praise her every single chance you get. When something bad about her pops into your mind, immediately replace the thought with one of her star qualities, especially if you were about to say something bad to her. And, ladies, live your marriage so that your man has plenty to brag about. Give him lots of ammunition. Raise your star qualities in his eyes to levels he cannot ignore. Marriage can be tough, but it's also exciting!

TIP

Watch closely for breaks, baitfish, and brush on your locator.

December 21

MATTHEW 6:14

"If you forgive others for their sins, your Father in heaven will also forgive you for your sins."

THIS IS THE TIME of the year to break out your "monster" spinnerbaits, those one ounce and heavier. I prefer nickel blades, and my favorite is solid white. Fish these baits deep with nonstretch line such as FireLine or Spiderwire. This will give you a great forgiving hookset, even in deep water.

TIP

Florida's best plastic worm colors are red shad and June bug.

Forgiveness is contagious. The more you forgive others, the more others will forgive you. It is also pretty easy once you start doing it. If you are harboring any type of malice, ill will, or hatred toward anyone today, simply forgive them. It doesn't really matter how much a person has wronged you, forgive them. You will feel better about them and about yourself, and God will ultimately be glorified.

December 22

LUKE 24:38

Jesus said, "Why are you troubled? Why do you doubt what you see?"

Bass fishermen, particularly tournament anglers, are known for getting help from one another. Even at the highest level, we continue to ask one another for help. We simply know that we don't have all the answers in every situation.

After Jesus' resurrection, many doubted and still did not believe what they were seeing. Some found it easier to believe they were seeing a ghost, not looking into the eyes of the risen Savior. But they were seeing Him, and we will also. Jesus is bigger than death, bigger than sickness, bigger than money problems, family problems, and work problems. He is bigger than any situation we will ever face. We need only to believe and not doubt what we see.

TIP
Trim and flare the weed guards on your jigs for better hookups.

December 23

ACTS 17:25

This God is the One who gives life, breath, and everything else to people. He does not need any help from them; he has everything he needs.

Why do so many fishermen give so much time, effort, and money teaching someone else how to be a better fisherman? Why do we give so much to kids—our own and others? Because we care about them? Yes, possibly, but also because giving to others makes us feel better. When we give, we usually receive even more.

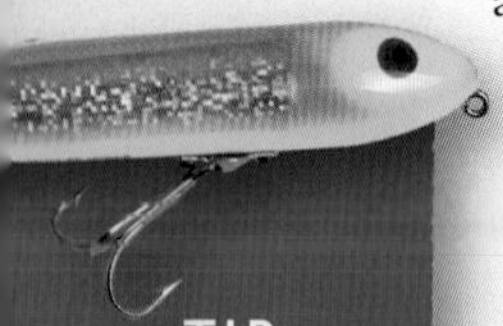

TIP

Frog pattern lures work well in small lakes and ponds.

God has designed our giving to Him as just another way to allow Him to help us. Again, we give, and we gain. Whether you are giving your time, your talents, or your money, God will use those to bless you even more. His interest is in your heart; His search is for your motives. When you really give out of the goodness of your heart, I believe you are making God happy.

DECEMBER 24

1 JOHN 3:6

So anyone who lives in Christ does not go on sinning.

ICE FISHING does not excite me. I have never tried ice fishing, so I cannot really say anything bad about it. But my real fear is that I might actually have a ball doing it. I know a lot of folks in the North who live for the day that the ice gets thick enough to venture out on.

I hate to sin. All Christians should hate to sin, but we all sin. So why do we venture into sin after Jesus has saved us? Because we do not live all of our lives in Christ. We are guilty of parceling out our lives to Jesus a little at a time. The parts we hold back are where we keep on sinning. God wants, even demands, that we turn ourselves completely over to Him. Only then can we really experience all the great riches He has for us.

TIP

To cut down the silhouette of a spinnerbait, remove ten or fifteen strands from the skirts.

December 25

REVELATION 22:17

Let whoever is thirsty come; whoever wishes may have the water of life as a free gift.

Big rains play havoc with fishing at any time of the year, but they can be particularly troubling in the winter. If the water is cold and gets muddy, the bite can get really hard. The solution can be simple. Go to the upper ends of creeks and rivers until you find clear water. Here you should be able to catch bass, crappie, white bass, walleye, or catfish.

TIP

Fish feed better and more often under a steady, normal barometer.

My Savior, Jesus, calls Himself "living water." He has poured Himself out on the cross as a sacrifice for you and me. We pay for water that we drink and use today, but the eternal life-giving water that is Jesus doesn't carry a price tag at all. It is free when you place your faith in Him.

DECEMBER 26

2 THESSALONIANS 1:10

This will happen on the day when the Lord Jesus comes to receive glory because of his holy people.

THIS IS THE TIME of the year when most tournament fishermen begin to look forward to the coming year. Whether you are fishing weekend tournaments in Oklahoma or Arkansas or fishing the BASS or FLW tour events, you are excited and building on the hope of a great year.

The day Jesus Christ returns to Earth is the great hope of all Christians. It is the hope that keeps us going through all the trials, persecutions, and problems we encounter along the way. This hope is real because of what Jesus has already done for us and is continuing to do on a daily basis. Never lose hope; never give up. One of the very best ways to keep your hope alive and strong is to share it with someone who doesn't have it.

TIP

Use smaller lures in ponds as most baitfish get eaten before they can mature.

December 27

PSALM 130:5

I wait for the Lord to help me,
and I trust his word.

I RECENTLY LISTENED to a five-year-old as he told me about going fishing and not even getting a single bite. I asked him how long he fished. With bright eyes and a dead serious look, he explained, "I fished five minutes and didn't catch anything."

TIP

Downsize your spinnerbaits and crankbaits when fishing current.

We've all been there. I suppose most of us might be there now with God. We covet God's help, we need God's help, but we want to set the terms. We want to draw up the deal, and we want that help—*now*. God's Word has the answer to any problem we need solved. The biggest problem any human can have is being lost without God, without Jesus. I guarantee that God can solve that problem, and He can absolutely do it—*now!*

December 28

PROVERBS 8:8

Everything I say is honest;
nothing I say is crooked or false.

THERE IS A SEASON for just about every type of lure. Deep into the colder months, most pros would recommend a jig or a slow-rolled spinnerbait. Good advice, but never be afraid of trying just about any lure in any situation. Remember that I have caught bass buzzing a spinnerbait in a snowstorm in December.

There is absolutely no season whatsoever for lying. Honesty is indeed the best policy. So much of our society is built around lying to one another, and we will forever be under God's condemnation as long as we continue that way. Think you don't lie? Tie a string around your finger today to remind you not to lie. See how many times you catch yourself rearranging the truth. Now, see how difficult it is to always talk the straight and narrow with your words.

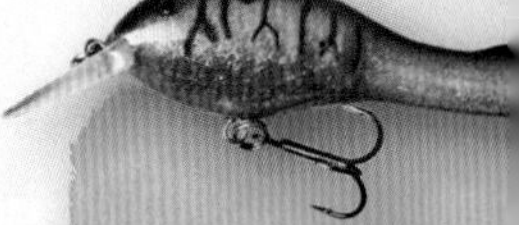

TIP

Store your outboard motor in the down position to prevent your lower unit from freezing.

December 29

2 CORINTHIANS 5:17

If anyone belongs to Christ, there is a new creation. The old things have gone; everything is made new!

WINTERTIME IS DOWNRIGHT DREARY. The coldness, dampness, and even grayness just seem to hang in the air. The longer the winter, the more we yearn for God to recreate our environment. We long for the dead-looking trees to turn green, the brown grass to disappear, the flowers to bloom, the gardens to be tempting with delicious vegetables. We long for the signs of new life. We long for God to warm the water and rejuvenate the fishing.

TIP

Never overlook a single stick-up or stump in open water flats.

Winter and springtime are pictures both of our lives and of what Jesus can do with us. He takes the cold, dark parts of our life in sin and turns us into the bright, smiling, loving, and forgiving new creations of His righteousness that He intends us to be.

DECEMBER 30

NEHEMIAH 9:20

You gave your good Spirit to teach them.

LEARNING TO FISH is a never-ending challenge. I know how to catch fish, yet I learn more every time I go. We cannot attain perfection in fishing.

So it is with our daily walk with Christ. We're saved, but not yet perfect. We will never know all the answers, but God has given each of us His Spirit to guide us through this life journey. Think of it: God's Spirit has the answers. Just as with fishing advice, though, we can choose whether or not to follow these instructions. Pay close attention to the Spirit's lessons for you today. You have within you the very best personal instructor to help you become the very best person you can be.

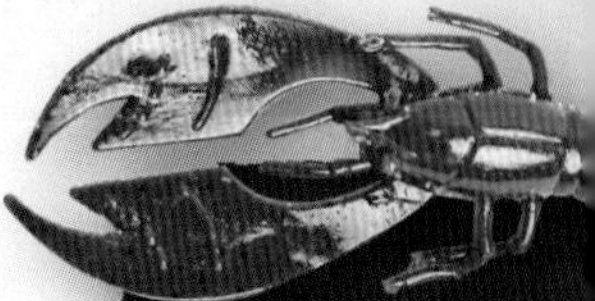

TIP

Light will penetrate the water about twice the depth at which you can see a white spinnerbait.

December 31

REVELATION 22:21

The grace of the Lord Jesus be with all.

THE LAST DAY OF THE YEAR to me is as exciting as the first as we look back upon what we have been through and look forward to what is to come.

The two are separated by 365 days, yet forever tied together by the simple stroke of the clock.

TIP

Take someone fishing! Enjoy God's great outdoors and share the love of Jesus with a friend.

Many times we feel so close, yet at other times, still so far away from Christ. But no matter how we feel, Jesus offered and paid for a relationship with us that will *never* end. He is always close to us. His direction and His purpose from God the Father was to establish that relationship with you and me. How very special we must be to God. How important our salvation must be to Him.

If you are saved, never take it for granted. If you are not saved, find someone today and ask them how you can be saved. May the grace of my Lord Jesus be with you forever.